Charles Sumner

Prophetic Voices Concerning America

A monograph

Charles Sumner

Prophetic Voices Concerning America
A monograph

ISBN/EAN: 9783337036812

Printed in Europe, USA, Canada, Australia, Japan

Cover: Foto ©ninafisch / pixelio.de

More available books at **www.hansebooks.com**

PROPHETIC VOICES

CONCERNING

AMERICA.

A MONOGRAPH.

BY

CHARLES SUMNER.

I have a far other and far brighter vision before my gaze. It may be but a vision, but I will cherish it. I see one vast confederation stretching from the frozen North in unbroken line to the glowing South, and from the wild billows of the Atlantic westward to the calmer waters of the Pacific main, — and I see one people, and one law, and one language, and one faith, and, over all that wide continent, the home of freedom, and a refuge for the oppressed of every race and of every clime. — JOHN BRIGHT, *Speech at Birmingham*, December 18, 1862: *Speeches by Rogers*, Vol. I. p. 225.

———————

BOSTON:
LEE AND SHEPARD, PUBLISHERS.
NEW YORK:
LEE, SHEPARD, AND DILLINGHAM.
1874.

THIS monograph appeared originally in the "Atlantic Monthly." It is now revised and enlarged. In the celebration of our hundredth birthday as a nation, now fast approaching, these prophetic voices will be heard, teaching how much of present fame and power was foreseen, also what remains to be accomplished.

C. S.

History shows that the civilization on which we depend is subject to a general law which makes it journey by halts, in the manner of armies, in the direction of the Occident, making the sceptre pass successively into the hands of nations more worthy to hold it, more strong and more able to employ it for the general good.

So it seems that the supreme authority is about to escape from Western and Central Europe, to pass to the New World. In the northern part of that other hemisphere offshoots of the European race have founded a vigorous society full of sap, whose influence grows with a rapidity that has never yet been seen anywhere. In crossing the ocean it has left behind on the soil of old Europe traditions, prejudices, and usages which, as *impediments* heavy to move, would have embarrassed its movements and retarded its progressive march. In about thirty years the United States will have, according to all probability, a hundred millions of population, in possession of the most powerful means, distributed over a territory which would make France fifteen or sixteen times over, and of the most wonderful disposition. . . .

Vainly do the occidental and central nations of Europe attribute to themselves a primacy which, in their vanity, they think sheltered from events and eternal; as if there were anything eternal in the grandeur and prosperity of societies, the works of men! — MICHEL CHEVALIER, *Rapports du Jury Internationel: Exposition Universelle de* 1867 *à Paris,* Tom. I., pp. dxiv. - dxvi.

America, and especially Saxon America, with its immense virgin territories, with its republic, with its equilibrium between stability and progress, with its harmony between liberty and democracy, is the continent of the future, — the immense continent stretched by God between the Atlantic and Pacific, where mankind may plant, essay, and resolve all social problems. [*Loud cheers.*] Europe has to decide whether she will confound herself with Asia, placing upon her lands old altars, and upon the altars old idols, and upon the idols immovable theocracies, and upon the theocracies despotic empires, or whether she will go by labor, by liberty, and by the republic, to collaborate with America in the grand work of universal civilization. — EMILIO CASTELAR, *Speech in the Spanish Cortes,* June 22, 1871.

MONOGRAPH.

THE discovery of America by Christopher Columbus is the greatest event of secular history. Besides the potato, the turkey, and maize, which it introduced at once for the nourishment and comfort of the Old World,[1] and also tobacco, which only blind passion for the weed could place in the beneficent group), this discovery opened the door to influences infinite in extent and beneficence. Measure them, describe them, picture them, you cannot. While yet unknown, imagination invested this continent with proverbial magnificence. It was the Orient and the land of Cathay. When afterwards it took a place in geography, imagination found another field in trying to portray its future history. If the Golden Age is before, and not behind, as is now happily the prevailing faith, then indeed must America share at least, if it does not monopolize, the promised good.

Before the voyage of Columbus in 1492, nothing of America was really known. Scanty scraps from antiq-

---

[1] In the Description of England, prefixed to Holinshed's Chronicles and dated 1586, one of these gifts is mentioned: "Of the potato and such venerous roots as are brought out of Spain, Portugal, and the Indies to furnish up our banquets, I speak not." Introduction, Book II., Chap. VI., Vol. I. p. 281. (London, 1807.)

nity, vague rumors from the resounding ocean, and the
hesitating speculations of science, were all that the inspired navigator found to guide him.   Foremost among
these were the well-known verses of Seneca, so interesting from ethical genius and a tragical death, in the chorus of his " Medea," which for generations had been the
finger-point to an undiscovered world.

> " . . . . venient annis
> Secula seris quibus Oceanus
> Vincula rerum laxet, et ingens
> Pateat tellus, Tiphys quo novos
> Detegat orbes, nec sit terris
> Ultima Thule." [1]

These verses are vague and lofty rather than specific ;
but Bacon, after setting them forth, says of them, " A
prophecy of the discovery of America"; and this they
may well be, if we adopt the translation of Archbishop
Whately, in his notes to the Essay on Prophecies :
"There shall come a time in later ages, when ocean
shall relax his chains and a vast continent appear, and
a pilot shall find new worlds, and Thule shall be no
more earth's bound."   Fox, turning from statesmanship
to scholarship, wrote to Wakefield : [2] "The prophecy in
Seneca's ' Medea ' is very curious indeed."   Irving says
of it : " Wonderfully apposite, and shows, at least, how
nearly the warm imagination of a poet may approach to
prophecy.   The predictions of the ancient oracle were
rarely so unequivocal." [3]   These verses were adopted by
Irving as a motto on the title-page of the revised edition of his " Life of Columbus."

---

[1] Act II., v. 371.

[2] June 20, 1800.   Memorials and Correspondence, by Lord John Russell,
Vol. IV. p. 393.

[3] Life of Columbus, Appendix, No. XXII., author's revised edition,
Vol. III. p. 402.

Four, if not more, copies are extant in the undoubted
handwriting of Columbus, — precious autographs to
tempt collectors; two in his work on the Prophecies,
another in a letter to Queen Isabella, and still another entered among his observations of lunar eclipses
at Hayti and Jamaica. By these the great admiral
sailed. Humboldt has preserved a copy in the following questionable form, without even mentioning the
variation in prosody and in an important word from
the received text: —

> " Venient annis secula seris
> Quibus Oceanus vincula rerum
> Laxet et ingens pateat tellus
> *Tethys* que novos detegat orbes
> Nec sit terris ultima Thule."

This is more curious, as the verses are correct in the
letter of Columbus, preserved by Navarrete.[1]

The sympathetic and authoritative commentator, who
has illustrated the enterprise with all that classical or
mediæval literature affords,[2] declares his conviction
that the discovery of a new continent was more completely foreshadowed in the simple geographical statement of the Greek Strabo, who, after a long life of
travel, sat down in the eighty-fourth year of his age, during the reign of Augustus, to write the geography of the
world, including its cosmography. In this work, where
are gathered the results of ancient study and experience,
the venerable author, after alluding to the possibility
of passing direct from Spain to India, and explaining
that the inhabited world is that which we inhabit and
know, thus lifts the curtain: "There may be in the

[1] Coleccion de los Viages y Descubrimientos. Tom. II. p. 272.
[2] Humboldt, Examen critique de la Géographie, Tom. I. pp. 101, 162.
See also Humboldt, Kosmos. Vol. II. pp. 516, 556, 557, 645.

same temperate zone *two and indeed more inhabited lands*, especially nearest the parallel of Thinæ or Athens, prolonged into the Atlantic Ocean." [1]   This was the voice of ancient science.

Before the voyage of Columbus two Italian poets seem to have beheld the unknown world.   The first was Petrarca ; nor was it unnatural that his exquisite genius should reach behind the veil of Time, as where he pictures

> " The daylight hastening with wingèd steps
> Perchance to gladden the expectant eyes
> *Of far-off nations in a world remote.*" [2]

The other was Pulci, who, in his *Morgante Maggiore*, sometimes called the last of the romances and the earliest of Italian epics, reveals an undiscovered world beyond the Pillars of Hercules.

> " Know that this theory is false; his bark
> The daring mariner shall urge far o'er
> The western wave, a smooth and level plain,
> Albeit the earth is fashioned like a wheel.
> Man was in ancient days of grosser mould,
> And Hercules might blush to learn how far
> Beyond the limits he had vainly set
> The dullest sea-boat soon shall wing her way.
>
> " *Men shall descry another hemisphere*,
> Since to one common centre all things tend;
> So earth, by curious mystery divine
> Well balanced, hangs amid the starry spheres.
> *At our Antipodes are cities, states,*
> *And throngèd empires, ne'er divined of yore.*
> But see, the sun speeds on his western path
> To glad the nations with expected light." [3]

This translation is by our own eminent historian,

----

[1] Lib. I. p. 65; Lib. II. p. 118.

[2] " . . . . che 'l dì nostro vola
A gente, che di là forse l' aspetta."
Canzone IV.

[3] Canto XXV. st. 229, 230.

Prescott, who first called attention to the testimony,[1] which is not mentioned even by Humboldt. Leigh Hunt referred to it at a later day.[2] Pulci was born in Florence, 1431, and died there, 1487, five years before Columbus sailed, so that he was not aided by any rumor of the discovery he so distinctly predicts.

Passing from the great event which gave a new world not only to Spain but to civilized man, it may not be uninteresting to collect some of the prophetic voices concerning the future of America and the vast unfolding of our continent. They will have a lesson also. Seeing what has been fulfilled, we may better judge what to expect. I shall set them forth in the order of time, prefacing each prediction with an account of the author sufficient to explain its origin and character. If some are already familiar, others are little known. Brought together in one body, on the principle of our national Union, *E pluribus unum*, they must give new confidence in the destinies of the Republic.

Only what has been said sincerely by those whose words are important deserves place in such a collection. Oracles had ceased before our history began, so that we meet no responses paltering in a double sense, like the deceptive replies to Crœsus and to Pyrrhus; nor any sayings which, according to the quaint language of Sir Thomas Browne, "seem quodlibetically constituted, and, like a Delphian blade, will cut both ways."[3] In Bacon's Essay on Prophecies there is a latitude not to be followed. Not fable or romance, but history, is the true

---

1 History of Ferdinand and Isabella, Vol. II. pp. 117, 118.

2 Stories from the Italian Poets, p 171.

3 Works, Vol. IV. p. 81 (edit. Pickering), Christian Morals.

authority, and here experience and genius are the lights
by which our prophets have walked. Doubtless there is
a difference in human faculties. Men who have lived
much and felt strongly see further than others. Their
vision penetrates the future. Second sight is little more
than clearness of sight. Milton tells us

> " That old experience does attain
>   To something like prophetic strain."

Sometimes this strain is attained even in youth. But
here Genius with divine power lifts the curtain and
sweeps the scene.

The elder Disraeli in his " Curiosities of Literature " has a chapter on " Prediction," giving curious
instances, among which is that of Rousseau, at the close
of the third book of "Émile," where he says, " We approach a condition of crisis and the age of revolutions." [1]
Our own Revolution was then at hand, soon followed
by that of France. The settlement of America was not
without auguries even at the beginning.

A PROPHETIC GROUP.

Before passing to the more serious examples I bring
into group a few, marking at least a poet's appreciation of the newly discovered country, if not a prophetic
spirit. The muse was not silent at the various reports.
As early as 1595, Chapman, famous as the translator of
Homer, in a poem on Guiana, thus celebrates and com-
mends the unknown land : —

> " Guiana, whose rich feet are mines of gold,
>   Whose forehead knocks against the roof of stars,
>   Stands on her tiptoe at fair England looking,

[1] Vol. III. p. 272.

Kissing her hand, bowing her mighty breast,
And every sign of all submission making,
To be the sister and the daughter both
Of our most sacred maid.

. . . . .

And there do palaces and temples rise
Out of the earth and kiss th' enamor'd skies,
Where new Britannia humbly kneels to Heaven,
The world to her, and both at her blest feet
In whom the circles of all empire meet."

In similar strain Drayton, who flourished under James I., addresses Virginia : —

" And ours to hold
Virginia,
Earth's only paradise.

" Where nature hath in store
Fowl, venison, and fish,
And the fruitful'st soil
Without your toil
Three harvests more,
All greater than your wish.

" To whose, the golden age
Still nature's laws doth give,
No other cares that 'tend
But them to defend
From winter's age,
That long there doth not live." [1]

Daniel, poet-laureate and contemporary, seemed to foresee the spread of our English speech, anticipating our own John Adams : —

" Who in time knows whither we may vent
The treasures of our tongue?   To what strange shores
This gain of our best glory shall be sent,
T' enrich unknowing nations with our stores?
What worlds, in the yet unformed Occident,
May 'come refined with th' accents that are ours?" [2]

[1] To the Virginian Voyage: Anderson's British Poets, Vol. III. p. 583.
[2] Musophilus: Anderson's British Poets, Vol. IV. p. 541.

The emigration prompted by conscience and for the
sake of religious liberty inspired the pious and poetical
Herbert to famous verses : —

> " Religion stands on tiptoe in our land,
> Ready to pass to the American straud."

The poet died in 1632, twelve years after the landing
of the Pilgrims at Plymouth, and only two years after
the larger movement of the Massachusetts Company,
which began the settlement of Boston. The verses saw
the light with difficulty, being refused the necessary
license ; but the functionary at last yielded, calling the
author " a divine poet," and expressing the hope that
" the world will not take him for an inspired prophet." [1]
Fuller, writing a little later, was perhaps moved by
Herbert when he said : " I am confident that America,
though the youngest sister of the four, is now grown
marriageable, and daily hopes to get Christ to her hus-
band, by the preaching of the gospel." [2]   In a different
vein a contemporary poet, the favorite of Charles I.,
Thomas Carew, in a masque performed by the monarch and his courtiers at Whitehall, February 18,
1633, made sport of New England, saying that it had
" purged more virulent humors from the politic body
than guaiacum and the West Indian drugs have from
the natural bodies of this kingdom." [3]   But these words
uttered at the English Court were praise.

Then came answering voices from the Colonies.   Rev.
William Morrill, of the Established Church, a settler of

---

[1] The Church Militant : Herbert's Poetical Works, p. 247, note (ed.
Little and Brown).

[2] The Holy State, Book III., Chap XVI., Of Plantations.

[3] Cœlum Britannicum : Anderson's British Poets, Vol. III. p. 716.

1623, said of New England, in a Latin poem translated by himself: —

"A grandchild to Earth's paradise is born,
Well limbed, well nerved, fair, rich, sweet, yet forlorn." [1]

"The Simple Cobbler of Agawam," another name for Rev. Nathaniel Ward of Ipswich, Mass., at the close of his witty book, first published in 1645 and having five different editions in the single year of 1647, sends an invitation to those at home : —

"So farewell England old
If evil times ensue,
Let good men come to us,
Wee 'l welcome them to New."

Another witness we meet in the writings of Franklin. It is George Webb, who, decamping from Oxford and the temptations of scholarship, indented himself according to the usage of the times, and became what Franklin calls "a bought servant" on our shores, where his genius flowered in the prophetic couplet, written in 1728 :—

"Rome shall lament her ancient fame declined,
And Philadelphia be the Athens of mankind."

Another English prophet, in verses written during our colonial days, foretells that his country shall see British wealth, power, and glory repeated in the New World:—

"In other lands, another Britain see,
And what thou art America shall be." [2]

And yet another, Hugh Henry Brackenridge, born in Scotland, and a graduate of our Princeton College in

---

[1] Duyckinck's Cyclopædia of American Literature, Vol. I. p. 2.
[2] Webster: Works, Vol. II. p. 510. Speech at the Festival of the Sons of New Hampshire.

1 *

1771, in a Commencement poem on "The Rising Glory
of America," pictured the future of the continent, adopt-
ing as a motto the verses of Seneca, so often quoted by
Columbus : —

> " This is thy praise, America, thy power,
> Thou best of climes by science visited,
> By freedom blest, and richly stored with all
> The luxuries of life. Hail, happy land,
> The seat of empire, the abode of kings,
> The final stage where Time shall introduce
> Renowned characters and glorious works of art,
> Which not the ravages of Time shall waste
> Till he himself has run his long career." [1]

To these add Voltaire, who, in his easy verse written
in 1751, represents God as putting fever in European climates "and the remedy in America." [2]

From this chorus, with only one discordant voice, I
pass to a long line of voices so distinct and full as to
be recognized separately.

JOHN MILTON, 1641.

The list opens with John Milton, whose lofty words
are like an overture to the great drama of emigration,
with its multitudes in successive generations. If not a
prophet, he has yet struck a mighty key-note in our history.

The author of " Paradise Lost," of "Comus" and the
heroic Sonnets, needs no special mention beyond the
two great dates of birth and death. He was born 9th

---

[1] Duyckinck's Cyclopædia of American Literature, Vol. I. p. 299.

[2] " Il met la fièvre en nos climats,
   Et le remède en Amérique."
   Epître au Roi de Prusse, LXXV.: Œuvres, XIII. p. 186 (ed. 1784).

December, 1608, and died 8th November, 1674. The treatise from which I quote was written in 1641.

"What numbers of faithful and free-born Englishmen and good Christians have been constrained to forsake their dearest home, their friends and kindred, whom nothing but the wide ocean and the savage deserts of America could hide and shelter from the fury of the bishops! O, if we could but see the shape of our dear mother England, as poets are wont to give a personal form to what they please, how would she appear, think ye, but in a mourning weed, with ashes upon her head, and tears abundantly flowing from her eyes, to behold so many of her children exposed at once and thrust from things of dearest necessity, because their conscience could not assent to things which the bishops thought indifferent? Let the astrologer be dismayed at the portentous blaze of comets and impressions in the air, as foretelling troubles and changes to states; I shall believe there cannot be a more ill-boding sign to a nation (God turn the omen from us!) than when the inhabitants, to avoid insufferable grievances at home, are enforced by heaps to forsake their native country." [1]

Here in a few words are the sacrifices made by our fathers, as they turned from their English homes, and also the conscience which prompted and sustained them. Begun in sacrifice and in conscience, their empire grew and flourished with constant and increasing promise of future grandeur.

ABRAHAM COWLEY, 1667.

Contemporary with Milton, and at the time a rival for the palm of poetry, was Abraham Cowley, born

[1] Reformation in England, Book II.: Works, Vol. III. p. 45 (Pickering's edition).

1618, died 28th July, 1667. His biography stands at
the head of Johnson's "Lives of the British Poets," the
first in that instructive collection. The two poets were
on opposite sides; Milton for the Commonwealth, Cowley for the King.

His genius was recognized in his own time, and when
he died, at the age of forty-nine, after a night of expos-
ure under the open sky, Charles II. said: "Mr. Cowley
has not left a better man behind him in England." He
was buried in Westminster Abbey, near Chaucer and
Spenser. But *post mortem* praise was too late to as-
suage the sting of royal ingratitude to a faithful servant.
His disappointment broke forth in the declared desire
"to retire to some of the American plantations and
forsake the world forever." Instead of America he selected the county of Kent, where he withdrew and especially delighted in the study of plants. His botany
flowered in poetry. He composed, in much admired
Latin verse, six books on Plants, — the first and second
in elegiac verse, displaying the qualities of herbs; the
third and fourth, in various measures, on the beauties of
flowers; and the fifth and sixth in hexameters, like the
Georgics, on the uses of trees. The first two books, in
Latin, appeared in 1662; the other four, also in Latin,
were not published till 1678, the year after his death.
They did not see the English light till 1705, when
a translation was published by Tate,[1] from which I
quote.

Two fruits of America are commemorated. The first
is that which becomes chocolate: —

[1] Cowley's History of Plants, a poem in six Books, with Rapin's Defi-
nition of Gardens, a poem in four Books. Translated from the Latin, the
former by N. Tate and others, the latter by James Gardner. (London, 1705.)

> " Guatimala produced a fruit unknown
> To Europe, which with double use endued
> For chocolate at once is drink and food,
> Does strength and vigor to the limbs impart,
> Makes fresh the countenance and cheers the heart." [1]

The other is the cocoa : —

> "While she preserves this Indian palm alone
> America can never be undone,
> Embowelled and of all her gold bereft
> Her liberty and cocas only left,
> She 's richer than the Spaniard with his theft." [2]

The poet, addressing the New World, becomes prophetic : —

> " To live by wholesome laws you now begin
> Buildings to raise and fence your cities in,
> To plough the earth, to plough the very main,
> And traffic with the universe maintain;
> Defensive arms and ornaments of dress,
> All implements of life you now possess.
> To you the arts of war and peace are known,
> And whole Minerva is become your own.
> Our muses, to your sires an unknown band,
> Already have got footing in your land.
> .   .   .   .   .

> "Long rolling years shall late bring on the times
> When with your gold debauched and ripened crimes
> Europe, the world's most noble part, shall fall
> Upon her banished gods and virtue call
> In vain, while foreign and domestic war
> At once shall her distracted bosom tear, —
> Forlorn, and to be pitied, even by you;
> *Meanwhile your rising glory you shall view,*
> *Wit, learning, virtue, discipline of war,*
> *Shall for protection to your world repair,*
> *And fix a long illustrious empire there.*
> .   .   .   .   .

> "Late destiny shall high exalt your reign,
> Whose pomp no crowds of slaves a needless train,
> Nor gold, the rabble's idol, shall support,

[1] Book V.   [2] Ibid.

Like Montezume's or Guanapaci's court,
But such true grandeur as old Rome maintained;
Where fortune was a slave, and virtue reigned." 1

This prophecy, though appearing in English tardily,
may be dated from 1667, when the Latin poem was
already written.

SIR THOMAS BROWNE, 1682.

Dr. Johnson called attention to a tract of Sir Thomas
Browne entitled "A Prophecy concerning the Future
State of Several Nations," where the famous author
"plainly discovers his expectation to be the same with
that entertained later with more confidence by Dr.
Berkeley, *that America will be the seat of the fifth empire*." 2 The tract is vague, but prophetic.

Sir Thomas Browne was born 19th October, 1605,
and died 19th October, 1682. His tract was published,
two years after his death, in a collection of Miscellanies,
edited by Dr. Tenison. As a much-admired author,
some of whose writings belong to our English classics,
his prophetic prolusions are not unworthy of notice.
They are founded on verses entitled "The Prophecy,"
purporting to have been sent him by a friend, among
which are the following: —

"When New England shall trouble new Spain,
When Jamaica shall be lady of the isles and the main;
When Spain shall be in America hid,
And Mexico shall prove a Madrid:
*When Africa shall no more sell out their blacks
To make slaves and drudges to the American tracts;*
.   .   .   .   .
*When America shall cease to send out its treasure,
But employ it at home in American pleasure;*

1 Book V.   2 Life of Sir Thomas Browne.

When the New World shall the Old invade,
Nor count them their lords but their fellows in trade;
    .   .   .   .
Then think strange things have come to light,
Whereof but few have had a foresight." [1]

Some of these words are striking, especially when we
consider their early date. The author of the " Religio
Medici " seems in the main to accept the prophecy,
which may be his own. In a commentary on each
verse he seeks to explain it. New England is "that
thriving colony which hath so much increased in his
day"; its people are already "industrious," and when
they have so far increased "that the neighboring country will not contain them, they will range still further,
and be able in time to set forth great armies, seek for
new possessions, or *make considerable and conjoined mi-
grations.*" The verse touching Africa will be fulfilled
" when African countries shall no longer make it a common trade to sell away their people." And this may
come to pass "whenever they shall be well civilized
and acquainted with arts and affairs sufficient to employ
people in their countries." It would also come to pass,
"if they should be converted to Christianity, but especially into Mahometism; for then they would never sell
those of their religion to be slaves unto Christians."
The verse concerning America is expounded thus:—

" That is, when America shall be better civilized, new
policied, and divided between great princes, it may come to
pass that they will no longer suffer their treasure of gold and
silver to be sent out to maintain the luxury of Europe and
other ports; but rather employ it to their own advantages,
in great exploits and undertakings, magnificent structures,
wars, or expeditions of their own." [2]

[1] Browne, Works, Vol. IV. pp. 232, 233.
[2] Ibid., p. 236.

The other verse, on the invasion of the Old World by the New, is explained : —

"That is, when America shall be so well peopled, civilized, and divided into kingdoms, *they are like to have so little regard of their originals as to acknowledge no subjection unto them;* they may also have a distinct commerce themselves, or but independently with those of Europe, and may hostilely and piratically assault them, even as the Greek and Roman colonies after a long time dealt with their original countries."[1]

That these speculations should arrest the attention of Dr. Johnson is something. They seem to have been in part fulfilled. An editor quietly remarks, that, "to judge from the course of events since Sir Thomas wrote, we may not unreasonably look forward to their more complete fulfilment."[2]

SIR JOSIAH CHILD AND DR. CHARLES DAVENANT, 1698.

In contrast with the poets, but mingling with them in forecast, were two writers on trade, who saw the future through facts and figures, or what one of them called "political arithmetic," even discerning colonial independence in the distance. These were Sir Josiah Child, born 1630 and died 1690, and Dr. Charles Davenant, born 1656 and died 1714.

Child is mentioned by Defoe as "originally a tradesman." Others speak of him as "a Southwalk brewer," and Macculloch calls him "one of the most extensive and, judging from his work, best-informed merchants

---

[1] Browne, Works, Vol. IV. p. 236.
[2] Ibid., p. 231, note.

of his time." [1]   He rose to wealth and consideration, founding a family which intermarried with the nobility. His son was known as Lord Castlemaine, Earl Tilney of Ireland. Davenant was eldest son of the author of Gondibert, "rare Sir William," and, like his eminent father, a dramatist. He was also member of Parliament, and wrote much on commercial questions ; but here he was less famous than Child, whose "New Discourse of Trade," so far as it concerned the interest of money, first appeared in 1668, and since then has been often reprinted and much quoted. There was an enlarged edition in 1694. That now before me appeared in 1698, and in the same year Davenant published his kindred "Discourses on the Public Revenues and on the Trade of England," among which is one "on the Plantation Trade." The two authors treated especially the Colonies, and in similar spirit.

The work of Child was brought to recent notice by the voluminous plodder George Chalmers, particularly in his writings on the Colonies and American Independence,[2] and then again by the elder Disraeli in his "Curiosities of Literature," who places a prophecy attributed to him in his chapter on "Prediction." After referring to Harrington and Defoe, "who ventured to predict an event, not by other similar events, but by a theoretical principle which he had formed," Disraeli quotes Chalmers : —

"Child, foreseeing from experience that men's *conduct* must finally be decided by their principles, FORETOLD the

[1] The Literature of Political Economy, p. 42.

[2] See Opinions on Interesting Subjects of Public Law and Commercial Policy arising from American Independence, p. 108. A motto on the reverse of the title-page is from Child.

B

colonial revolt. Defoe, allowing his prejudices to obscure
his sagacity, reprobated that suggestion, because he deemed
interest a more strenuous prompter than enthusiasm."

The pleasant hunter of curiosities then says : —

"The predictions of Harrington and Defoe are precisely
such as we might expect from a petty calculator or a political economist, who can see nothing further than immediate
results ; but the true philosophical predictor was Child, who
had read the *past.*" [1]

D'Israeli was more curious than accurate. His ex-
cuse is that he followed another writer.[2] The prediction attributed to Child belongs to Davenant; but the
two are coupled by the introduction of words from the
former.

The work of Child is practical rather than speculative, and shows a careful student of trade. Dwelling
on the " plantations " of England and their value, he
considers their original settlement, and here we find a
painful contrast between New England and Virginia.[3]
Passing from the settlement to the character, New
England is described as " being a more independent
government from this kingdom than any other of our
plantations, and the people that went thither more one
peculiar sort or sect than those that went to the rest of
our plantations." [4] He recognized in them "a people,
whose frugality, industry, and temperance, and the happiness of whose laws and institutions, do promise to
themselves long life with *a wonderful increase of peo-*

1 Curiosities of Literature, Vol. III. p. 303·(ed. London, 1849).
2 Chalmers, Life of Defoe, p. 68.
3 A New Discourse of Trade, p. 183 (ed. 1698).
4 Ibid., p. 201.

ple, riches, and power." [1]   And then: "Of all the American plantations, his Majesty hath none so apt for the building of shipping as New England. Nor none comparably so qualified for breeding of seamen, not only by reason of the natural industry of that people, but principally by reason of their cod and mackerel fisheries." [2]   On his last page are words more than complimentary : —

"To conclude this chapter and to do right to that most industrious English colony, I must confess that though we lose by their unlimited trade with our foreign plantations, yet we are very great gainers by their direct trade to and from Old England.   Our yearly English exportations of English manufactures, malt and other goods from hence thither, amounting in my opinion to ten times the value of what is imported from thence." [3]

Here is keen observation, but hardly prophecy.

Contrast this with Davenant : —

"As the case now stands, we shall show that they [the Colonies] are a spring of wealth to this nation, that they work for us, that their treasure centres all here, and that the laws have tied them fast enough to us ; so that it must be through our own fault and misgovernment, *if they become independent of England. . . . .* Corrupt governors may hereafter provoke them to withdraw their obedience, and by supine negligence or upon mistaken measures, we may let them grow, more especially New England, in naval strength and power, *which, if suffered, we cannot expect to hold them long in our subjection.*   If, as some have proposed, we should think to build ships of war there, we may teach them an art which

---

[1] A New Discourse of Trade, p. 203 (ed. 1698).

[2] Ibid., p. 215.

[3] Ibid., p. 216.

will cost us some blows to make them forget. Some such courses may, indeed, drive them, or put it into their heads, *to erect themselves into independent Commonwealths.*" [1]

Davenant then quotes Child's remark on New England as "the most proper for building ships and breeding seamen," and adds : —

"So that, if we should go to cultivate among them the art of navigation and teach them to have a naval force, *they may set up for themselves and make the greatest part of our West India trade precarious.*" [2]

These identical words are quoted by Chalmers, who exclaims : "Of that prophecy we have lived, alas! to see the fulfilment." [3] Doubtless, on this Disraeli founded his prediction.

Chalmers emigrated from Scotland to Maryland, and practised in the colonial courts, but, disgusted with American independence, returned home, where he wrote · and edited much, especially on colonial questions, ill concealing a certain animosity, and, on one occasion, stating that, among the documents in the Board of Trade and Paper Office were "the most satisfactory proofs" of the settled purpose of the Colonies, from "the epoch of the Revolution of 1688," "to acquire direct independence." [4] But none of these proofs are presented. The same allegation was also made by Viscount Bury in his "Exodus of Western Nations," [5] but also without proofs.

The name of Defoe is always interesting, and I can-

1 Discourses, Part II. pp. 204, 205.
2 Ibid., p. 206.
3 Opinions on Interesting Subjects, p. 109.
4 Opinions of Eminent Lawyers, Preface xvi.
5 Vol. II. p. 395.

not close this article without reference to the saying attributed to him by D'Israeli. I know not where in his multitudinous writings it may be found, unless in his " Plan of the English Commerce," and here careful research discloses nothing nearer than this : —

" What a glorious trade to England it would be to have these colonies increased with a million of people, to be clothed, furnished, and supplied with all their needful things, food excepted, only from us, and *tied down forever to us by that immortal, indissoluble bond of trade, their interest.*" [1]

In the same work he says : —

" This is certain and will be granted, that the product of our improved colonies raises infinitely more trade, employs more hands, and, I think I may say by consequence, brings in more wealth to this one particular nation or people, the English, than all the mines of New Spain do to the Spaniards." [2]

In this vision the author of Robinson Crusoe was permitted to see the truth with regard to our country, although failing to recognize future independence.

BISHOP BERKELEY, 1726.

It is pleasant to think that Berkeley, whose beautiful verses predicting the future of America are so often quoted, was so sweet and charming a character. Atterbury wrote of him : " So much understanding, knowledge, innocence, and humility I should have thought confined to angels, had I never seen this gentleman." Swift said : " He is

---

[1] Page 361.
[2] Ibid., pp 306, 307. See also The Complete English Tradesman, Chap. XXXVI., Works, Vol. XVII. pp. 256, 259.

an absolute philosopher with regard to money, title, and power." Pope let drop a tribute which can never die,—

"To Berkeley every virtue under Heaven."

Such a person was naturally a seer.

He is compendiously called an Irish prelate and philosopher. Born in Kilkenny, 1684, and dying in Oxford, 1753, he began as a philosopher. While still young, he wrote his famous treatise on "The Principles of Human Knowledge," where he denies the existence of matter, insisting that it is only an impression produced on the mind by Divine power. After travel for several years on the Continent, and fellowship with the witty and learned at home, among whom were Addison, Swift, Pope, Garth, and Arbuthnot, he conceived the project of educating the aborigines of America, which was set forth in a tract, published in 1725, entitled "Scheme for Converting the Savage Americans to Christianity by a College to be erected in the Summer Islands, otherwise called the Isles of Bermuda." Persuaded by his benevolence, the ministers promised twenty thousand pounds, and there were several private subscriptions to promote what was called by the king "so pious an undertaking.". Berkeley possessed already a deanery in Ireland, with one thousand pounds a year. Turning away from this residence, and refusing to be tempted by an English mitre, offered by the queen, he set sail for Rhode Island, "which lay nearest Bermuda," where, after a tedious passage of five months, he arrived 23d January, 1729. Here he lived on a farm back of Newport, having been, according to his own report, "at great expense for land and stock." In familiar letters he has recorded his impression of this place, famous since for fashion. "The climate," he says, " is like that of Italy, and not at all colder in the winter than I have known it everywhere north of Rome. This island is pleasantly laid out in hills and vales and rising grounds, hath plenty of excellent springs and fine rivulets and many delightful landscapes of rocks and promontories and adjacent lands. The town of Newport contains about six thousand souls, and is the most thriving, flourishing place in all America for its bigness. It is very pretty and pleasantly situated. I was never more agreeably surprised than at the first sight of the town and its harbor." [1] He seems to have been contented, and when his companions went to Boston stayed at home, " preferring," as he wrote, " quiet and solitude to the noise of a great town, notwithstanding all the solicitations that have been used to draw us thither." [2]

The money he had expected, especially from the king's ministers, failed, and after waiting in vain expectation two years and a half, he returned to England, leaving an infant son buried in the churchyard of Trinity, and bestowing upon Yale College a library of eight hundred and eighty volumes, as well as his estate in Rhode Island. During his residence at Newport he had preached every Sunday, and was indefatigable in pastoral duties, besides meditating, if not composing, "The Minute Philosopher," which was published shortly after his return.

In his absence he had not been forgotten at home; and shortly after his return he became Bishop of Cloyne, in which place he was most exemplary, devoting himself to his episcopal duties, to the education of his children, and the pleasures of composition.

1 Berkeley, Works, Vol. I., Life prefixed, p. 53.
2 Ibid., p. 55.

It was while occupied with his plan of a college, especially as a nursery for the Colonial churches, shortly before sailing for America, that the great future was revealed to him, and he wrote the famous poem, the only one found among his works, entitled "Verses on the Prospect of Planting Arts and Learning in America."[1] The date may be fixed at 1726. Such a poem was an historic event. I give the first and last stanzas.

> " The Muse, disgusted at an age and clime
> Barren of every glorious theme,
> *In distant lands now waits a better time,*
> *Producing subjects worthy fame.*
>
> .   .   .   .   .
>
> *Westward the course of empire takes its way ;*
> The first four acts already past,
> A fifth shall close the drama with the day ;
> Time's noblest offspring is the last."

It is difficult to exaggerate the value of these verses, which have been so often quoted as to become a commonplace of literature and politics. There is nothing from any oracle, there is very little from any prophecy, which can compare with them. The biographer of Berkeley, who wrote in the last century, was very cautious, when, after calling them "a beautiful copy of verses," he says that "another age will perhaps acknowledge the old conjunction of the prophetic character with that of the poet to have again taken place."[2] The *vates* of the Romans was poet and prophet ; and such was Berkeley.

Mr. Webster calls this an "extraordinary prophecy," and then says : " It was an intuitive glance into futurity ; it was a grand conception, strong, ardent, glowing, embracing all time since the creation of the world and all

---

[1] Berkeley, Works, Vol. II. p. 443.
[2] Ibid., Vol. I., Life prefixed, p. 15.

regions of which that world is composed, and judging of the future by just analogy with the past. And the inimitable imagery and beauty with which the thought is expressed, joined to the conception itself, render it one of the most striking passages in our language." [1]

The sentiment which prompted the prophetic verses of the excellent Bishop was widely diffused, or perhaps it was a natural prompting.[2] Of this illustration is afforded in the life of Benjamin West. On his visit to Rome in 1760, the young artist encountered a famous improvvisatore, who, learning that he was an American come to study the fine arts in Rome, at once addressed him with the ardor of inspiration, and to the music of his guitar. After singing the darkness which for so many ages veiled America from the eyes of science, and also the fulness of time when the purposes for which this continent had been raised from the deep would be manifest, he hailed the youth before him as an instrument of Heaven to raise there a taste for the arts which elevate man, and an assurance of refuge to science and knowledge, when, in the old age of Europe, they should have forsaken her shores. Then, in the spirit of prophecy, he sang : —

"*But all things of heavenly origin, like the glorious sun, move westward ; and truth and art have their periods of shining and of night. Rejoice then, O venerable Rome, in thy divine destiny ; for though darkness overshadow thy seats, and though thy mitred head must descend into the dust, thy spirit immortal and undecayed already spreads towards a new world.*"[3]

1 Address at the laying of the corner-stone of the addition to the Capitol, July 4, 1851: Works, Vol. II. p. 596. See also p. 510.
2 Grahame, History of the United States, Vol. IV. pp. 136, 448.
8 Galt, Life of West, Vol. I. pp. 116, 117.

2

John Adams in his old age, dwelling on the reminiscences of early life, records that nothing was "more ancient in his memory than the observation that arts, sciences, and empire had travelled westward, and in conversation it was always added, since he was a child, that their next leap would be over the Atlantic into America." With the assistance of an octogenarian neighbor, he recalled a couplet that had been repeated with rapture as long as he could remember : —

> "The Eastern nations sink, their glory ends,   .
> And empire rises where the sun descends."

It was imagined by his neighbor that these lines came from some of our early pilgrims, — by whom they had been "inscribed, or rather drilled, into a rock on the shore of Monument Bay in our old Colony of Plymouth."[1]

Another illustration of this same sentiment is found in Burnaby's "Travels through the Middle Settlements of North America, in 1759 and 1760," a work first published in 1775. In reflections at the close the traveller remarks : —

> "An idea, strange as it is visionary, has entered into the minds of the generality of mankind, *that empire is travelling westward : and every one is looking forward with eager and impatient expectation to that destined moment when America is to give the law to the rest of the world.*"[2]

The traveller is none the less an authority for the prevalence of this sentiment because he declares it "illusory and fallacious," and records his conviction that

---

[1] Works, Vol. IX. pp. 597 – 599.
[2] Burnaby, Travels, p. 115.

"America is formed for happiness, but not for empire." Happy America! What empire can compare with happiness! Making amends for this admission, the jealous traveller, in his edition of 1796, after the adoption of the National Constitution, announces that "the present union of American States will not be permanent, or last for any considerable length of time," and "that that extensive country must necessarily be divided into separate states and kingdoms."[1] Thus far the Union has stood against all shocks, foreign or domestic; and the prophecy of Berkeley is more than ever in the popular mind.

SAMUEL SEWALL, 1727.

Berkeley saw the sun of empire travelling westward. A contemporary whose home was made in New England, Samuel Sewall, saw the New Heaven and the New Earth. He was born at Bishop-Stoke, England, 28th March, 1652, and died at Boston, 1st January, 1730. A child emigrant in 1661, he became a student and graduate of our Cambridge; in 1692, Judge of the Supreme Court of Massachusetts; in 1718, Chief Justice. He was of the court which condemned the witches, but afterwards, standing up before the congregation of his church, made public confession of error, and his secret diary bears testimony to his trial of conscience. In harmony with this contrition was his early feeling for the enslaved African, as witness his tract "The Selling of Joseph," so that he may be called the first of our Abolitionists.

Besides an "Answer to Queries respecting America," in 1690, and "Proposals touching the Accomplishment

---

[1] Burnaby, Travels, Preface, p. 21.

of the Prophecies," in 1713, he wrote another work, with the following title : —

"Phænomena quædam Apocalyptica ad Aspectum Novi Orbis configurata. Or some few Lines towards a description of the New Heaven as it makes to those who stand upon the New Earth, By Samuel Sewall A. M. and some time Fellow of Harvard College at Cambridge in New England."

The copy before me is the second edition, with the imprint, "Massachuset, Boston Printed by Bartholomew Green, & sold by Benjamin Eliot, Samuel Gerrish & Daniel Henchman, 1727." There is a prophetic voice even in the title, which promises "some few lines towards a description of the New Heaven as it makes to those who stand upon the New Earth." This is followed by verses from the Scriptures, among which is Isaiah xi. 14: "But they shall fly upon the shoulders of the Philistines toward the west"; also, Acts i. 8 : "Ye shall be witnesses unto me unto the uttermost parts of the earth," — quoting here from the Spanish Bible, *Hasta lo ultimo de la tierra.*

In the second Dedication the author speaks of his book as "this vindication of America." Then comes, in black letter, what is entitled "Psalm, 139, 7 – 10," containing this stanza : —

> " Yea, let me take the morning wings
> And let me go and hide,
> Even there where are the farthest parts
> Where flowing sea doth slide.
> Yea, even thither also shall
> Thy reaching hand me guide;
> And thy right hand shall hold me fast,
> And make me to abide."

Two different dedications follow, the first dated " Boston, N. E., April 16th, 1697." Here are words on the same key with the title: —

"For I can't but think that either England or New England, or both together is best, is the only bride-maid mentioned by name in David's Epithalamium to assist at the great wedding now shortly to be made. . . . . Angels incognito have sometimes made themselves guests to men, designing thereby to surprise them with a requital of their love to strangers. In like manner the English nation in showing kindness to the aboriginal natives of America may possibly show kindness to Israelites unaware. . . . . Instead of being branded for slaves with hot irons in the face and arms, and driven by scores in mortal chains, they shall wear the name of God in their foreheads, and they shall be delivered into the glorious liberty of the children of God. . . . . Asia, Africa, and Europe have each of them had a glorious gospel-day. None, therefore, will be grieved at any one's pleading that America may be made coparcener with her sisters in the free and sovereign grace of God."

Entering upon his subject, our prophet says: —

"Whereas *New-England*, and *Boston* of the *Massachusets* have this to make mention of; that they can tell their Age, and account it their Honour to have their birth, and parentage kept in everlasting remembrance. And in every deed, the families, and churches which first ventured to follow Christ thorow the *Atlantick* Ocean, into a strange land, full of wild men, were so religious ; their end so holy ; their self-denyal in pursuing of it, so extraordinary ; that I can't but hope that the plantation has thereby gaind a very strong Crasis ; and that it will not be of one or two, or three centuries only ; but by the Grace of God it will be very long lasting."[1]

[1] Page 1.

Then again : —

" New-Jerusalem will not straiten, and enfeeble ; but won-
derfully dilate, and invigorate Christianity in the several
Quarters of the World, in Asia, in Africa, in Europe, and in
America. And one that has been born, or but liv'd in
America, more than three score years ; it may be pardon-
able for him to ask, Why may not that be the place of New-
Jerusalem."[1]

And here also : —

" Of all the parts of the world, which do from this Charter, entitle themselves to the Government of Christ, America's
plea, in my opinion is the strongest. For when once Christopher *Columbus* had added this fourth to the other *three*
parts of the foreknown World ; they who sailed farther
Westward, arriv'd but where they had been before. The
Globe now failed of offering any thing New to the adventurous Travailer : or however, it could not afford another
new World. And probably, the consideration of *America's*
being *the beginning of the East, and the End of the West;* was
that which moved Columbus to call some part of it by the
Name of Alpha and Omega. Now if the last Adam did give
order for the engraving of his own name upon this last
Earth : 'twill draw with it great Consequences ; even such
as will, in time, bring the poor Americans out of their
Graves, and make them live."[2]

Again he says : —

" May it not with more or equal strength be argued New
Jerusalem is not the same with Jerusalem : but as Jerusalem was to the westward of Babylon, so New Jerusalem
must be to the westward of Rome, to avoid disturbance in
the order of mysteries."[3]

[1] Pages 1, 2,   [2] Pages 2, 3.   [3] Page 31.

Then quoting the English verses of Herbert, and the Latin verses of Cowley, he says: " Not doubting but that these authorities, being brought to the king's scales, will be over weight."[1]

Afterwards he adduces " learned Mr. Nicholas Fuller," who would have it believed that America was first peopled " by the posterity of our great-grandfather Japheth, though he will not be very strict with us as to the particular branch of that wide family." The extract from this new authority is remarkable for its vindication to Columbus of the name of the new Continent. " Quam passim Americam dicunt, vere ac merito Columbinam potius dicerent, a magnanimo heroe Christophoro Columbo Gennensi primo terrarum illarum investigatore atque inventore plane divinitus constituto."[2] This designation he adopts in his own text: thus, " Hinc ergo Columbina primum ";[3] then again, " Multo is quidem proprior est Columbina ";[4] then again, " America seu verius Columbina ";[5] then again, " Repertam fuisse Columbinam."[6] This effort draws from our prophet a comment: —

"But why should a learned Man make all this *Dirige* for Columbus's Name! What matter is it how America be called? For Flavio of Malphi in Naples hath, in great

---

1 Page 34.

2 "Which everywhere they call America ; truly and deservedly they should say rather Columbina from the magnanimous hero Christopher Columbus, the Genoese, first explorer, and plainly divinely appointed discoverer of these lands." — *Miscell. Sac.*, Lib, II. cap. 4 in fine. See also cap. 84 and 85.

3 " Hence, therefore, Columbina first."

4 " It is indeed much nearer to Columbina."

5 " America, or more truly Columbina."

6 " That Columbina would be found."

measure, applied the vertues of the loadstone to the
Mariners Compass in Vain; the Portugals have found the
length of Africa's foot in Vain; the Spaniards sent out
the Italian Dove, in Vain; Sir *Francis Drake* hath sailed
round the world, and made thorow Lights to it, in Vain;
and Hackluyt and Purchas have, with endless Labour, acquainted Englishmen with these things in Vain: If after
all, we go about to turn the American Euphrates into a
Stygian Lake! The breaking of this One Instrument, spoils
us of the long expected, and much desired, Consort of Mu-
sick."[1]

Very soon thereafter he breaks forth in words, printed
in large Italic type and made prophetic: —

" *Lift up your heads, O ye Gates* [of Columbina], *and
be ye lift up, ye Everlasting Doors, and the KING of Glory
shall come in.*"

MARQUIS D'ARGENSON, 1745.

From the Puritan son of New England, pass now to
a different character. René Louis de Voyer, Marquis
d'Argenson, a French noble, was born 18th October,
1694, and died 26th January, 1757, so that his life
lapped upon the prolonged reigns of Louis XIV. and
Louis XV. At college the comrade of Voltaire, he was
ever afterwards the friend and correspondent of this
great writer. His own thoughts, commended by the
style of the other, would have placed him among the
most illustrious of French history. Notwithstanding
strange eccentricities, he was often elevated, far-sighted,
and prophetic, above any other Frenchman except Tur-

[1] Page 50.

got. By the courtiers of Versailles he was called "the stupid" (*la bête*), while Rousseau hailed one of his productions, yet in manuscript, as "the work of Aristides." The Duke of Richelieu, borrowing perhaps from Voltaire, called him "Secretary of State for the Republic of Plato"; and the latter pronounced him "the first citizen who had ever reached the ministry."

Except a brief subordinate service and two years of the Cabinet as Minister of Foreign Affairs, his life was passed in meditation and composition, especially on subjects of government and human improvement. This was his great passion. "If being in power," he wrote, "I knew a capable man, I would go on all fours to seek him, to pray him to serve me as counsellor and tutor."[1] Is not this a lesson to the heedless partisan?

He was an active member of a small club devoted to hardy speculation, commencing in 1725, and known, from its place of meeting at the apartment of one of its members, as *l'Entre-Sol*. It is to his honor that he mingled here with Abbé Saint-Pierre, and sympathized entirely with the many-sided, far-sighted plans of this "good man." In the privacy of his journal he records his homage: "This worthy citizen is not known, and he does not know himself. . . . . He has much intelligence, and has given himself to a kind of philosophy profound and abandoned by everybody, which is true politics destined to procure the greatest happiness of men."[2] In praising Saint-Pierre our author furnished a measure of himself.

The work which excited the admiration of Rousseau was *Considérations sur le Gouvernement ancien et présent de la France*, which was read by Voltaire as early as

---

[1] Journal et Mémoires, Tom. I. p. xlvii., Introduction.
[2] Ibid., Feb., 1734, Tom. I. p. 155.

1739, but did not see the light till some years after the
death of the author. It first appeared at Amsterdam in
1764, and in a short time there were no less than four
editions in Holland. In 1784 and 1787 a more accurate edition appeared in France, and soon another at the
command and expense of the Assembly of Notables.
Here was a recognition of the people and an inquiry
how far democracy was consistent with monarchical
government. Believing much in the people and anxious for their happiness, he had not ceased to believe
in kings. The book was contained in the epigraph
from the *Britannicus* of Racine : —

> " Que dans le cours d'un regne florissant,
>   *Rome soit toujours libre,* et Cæsar tout-puissant."

Other works followed, some of which are still in
manuscript, and others were published tardily, as the
"Journal and Memoirs," in eight volumes; "Essays
in the Style of those of Montaigne"; "Memoirs of
State"; "Foreign Affairs, containing Memoirs of my
Ministry"; "Remarks while Reading"; and especially,
"Thoughts on the Reformation of the State";[1] also,
"Thoughts since my Leaving the Ministry." In all
these there is a communicativeness like that of Saint
Simon in his Memoirs, and of Rousseau in his Confes-
sions, without the wonderful talent of either. The advanced ideas of the author are constantly conspicuous,
making him foremost among contemporaries in discerning the questions of the future. Even of marriage
he writes in the spirit of some modern reformers : "It is
necessary to press the people to marriage, *waiting for
something better.*" This is an instance. His reforms

[1] Pensées sur la Reformation de l'Etat, 2 vols. in 4to.

embraced nothing less than the suppression of feudal
privileges and of the right of primogeniture, uniformity
of weights and measures, judges irremovable and salaried
by the State, the dismissal of foreign troops, and the
residence of the king and his ministers in the capital
embellished by vast squares, pierced by broad streets,
"with the *bois de Boulogne* for country." This is the
Paris of latter days. Add to this the suppression of
cemeteries, hospitals, and slaughter-houses in the interior
of Paris, and many other things, omitting omnibuses but
including balloons. "Here is something," he records,
"which will be treated as folly. I am persuaded that
one of the first famous discoveries to make, and reserved
perhaps for our age, is to find the art of flying in the
air." And he proceeds to describe the balloon.[1]

His large nature is manifest in cosmopolitan ideas, and
the inquiry if it were not well to consider one's self "as
citizen of the world," more than is the usage. Here his
soul glows :—

"What a small corner Europe has on the round earth !
What lands remain to inhabit ! See this immense extent of
three parts of the world, and of undiscovered lands at the
north and south ! If people went there with other views
than that disagreeable exclusive property, all these lands
would be inhabited in two centuries. We shall not see this,
but it will come." [2]

And then, after coupling morals and well-being, he
announces the true rule : "An individual who shall do
well will succeed, and who shall do ill will fail ; *it is
the same with nations.*" This is just and lofty. In such

---

1 Journal et Mémoires, Tom. I. p. liv., Introduction.
2 Ibid., p. xxxiii., Introduction.

a spirit he cherished plans of political reconstruction in
foreign nations, especially in Italy. The old Italian cry
was his : " The barbarians must be driven from Italy ";
and he contemplated " one Republic or eternal association of Italian powers, as there was one German, one
Dutch, one Helvetic," and he called this " the greatest
affair that had been treated in Europe for a long time." [1]
The entry of Italy was to be closed to the Emperor; and
he adds : " For ourselves what a happy privation, if we
are excluded forever from the necessity of sending there
our armies to triumph, but to perish." [2]

The intelligence that saw Italy so clearly saw France
also, and her exigencies, marking out " a national senate
composed equally of all the orders of the state," and
which, on questions of peace and war, would hold the
kings in check by the necessity of obtaining supplies " ; [3]
also saw the approaching decay of Turkey, and wished
to make Greece flourishing once more, to acquire possession of the holy places, to overcome the barbarians of
Northern Africa by a union of Christian powers, which
" well united once in a kind of Christian Republic, according to the project of Henry the Fourth, detailed by
the Abbé Saint-Pierre, would have something better to
do than to fight to destroy each other as they do."
Naturally this singular precocious intelligence reached
across the Atlantic, and here he became one of our
prophets.

" Another great event to arrive upon the round earth
is this.   The English have in Northern America domains

---

[1] Sainte Beuve, Causeries du Lundi, Tom. XII. p. 105 : Le Marquis
d'Argenson.

[2] Journal et Mémoires, p. xxxvii., Introduction.

[3] Ibid., p. 363, Appendix.

great, strong, rich, well regulated.   There are in New England a parliament, governors, troops, white inhabitants in abundance, riches, and mariners, which is worse.

"I say that some bright morning these dominations can separate from England, rise and erect themselves into an independent republic.

"What will happen from this?   Do people think of this? A country well regulated by the arts of Europe, in condition to communicate with it by the present perfection of its marine, and which by this will appropriate our arts in proportion to their improvement; patience!   Such a country in several ages will make great progress in population and in politeness; such a country will render itself in a short time master of America, and especially of the gold-mines."[1]

Then, dwelling on the extension of commercial liberty and the improvement of the means of communication, he exclaims, with lyrical outburst: —

"And you will then see how the earth will be beautiful! What culture!   What new arts and new sciences!   What safety for commerce!   Navigation will precipitate all the peoples towards each other.   A day will come when one will go in a populous and regulated city of California as one goes in the stage-coach of Meaux."[2]

The published works of D'Argenson do not enable us to fix the precise date of these remarkable words.   They are from the "Thoughts on the Reformation of the State," but these extend over a long period of time, beginning as early as 1733, while his intimacy with the Abbé Saint-Pierre was at its height.   Placing them mid-

[1] Pensées sur la Réformation de l'État: Journal et Mémoires, Introduction, lv, lvi.

[2] Ibid., lvi.

way between the earliest entry of that work and his death, their date may be 1745, during his ministry, thus preceding Turgot and John Adams. But each spoke from his own soul and without prompting.

TURGOT, 1750, 1770, 1776, 1778.

AMONG the illustrious names of France few equal that of Turgot. He was a philosopher among ministers, and a minister among philosophers. Malesherbes said of him, that he had the heart of L'Hôpital and the head of Bacon. Such a person in public affairs was an epoch for his country and for the human race. Had his spirit prevailed, the bloody drama of the French Revolution would not have occurred, or it would at least have been postponed. I think it could not have occurred. He was a good man, who sought to carry into government the rules of goodness. His career from beginning to end was one continuous beneficence. Such a nature was essentially prophetic, for he discerned the natural laws by which the future is governed.

He was of an ancient Norman family, whose name suggests the god Thor; he was born at Paris, 1727, and died, 1781. Being a younger son, he was destined for the Church, and commenced his studies as an ecclesiastic at the ancient Sorbonne. Before registering an irrevocable vow, he announced his repugnance to the profession, and turned aside to other pursuits. Law, literature, science, humanity, government, now engaged his attention. He associated himself with the authors of the Encyclopædia, and became one of its contributors. In other writings he vindicated especially the virtue of toleration. Not merely a theorist, he soon

arrived at the high post of Intendant of Limousin, where
he developed talent for administration and sympathy
with the people. The potato came into that province
through him. But he continued to employ his pen,
especially on questions of political economy, which he
treated as a master. On the accession of Louis XVI.
he was called to the cabinet as Minister of the Marine,
and shortly afterwards gave up this place to be the head
of the finances. Here he began a system of rigid economy, founded on curtailment of expenses and enlarge-
ment of resources. The latter was obtained especially
by removal of disabilities from trade, whether at home
or abroad, and the substitution of a single tax on land
for a complex multiplicity of taxes. The enemies of
progress were too strong at that time, and the king dis-
missed the reformer. Good men in France became
anxious for the future; Voltaire, in his distant retreat,
gave a shriek of despair, and addressed to Turgot remarkable verses entitled *Épître à un Homme*. Worse
still, the good edicts of the minister were rescinded, and
society was put back.   .

The discarded minister gave himself to science, literature, and friendship. He welcomed Franklin to
France and to immortality in a Latin verse of marvellous felicity. He was already the companion of the
liberal spirits who were doing so much for knowledge
and for reform. By writing and by conversation he
exercised a constant influence. His " ideas " seem to
illumine the time. We may be content to follow him
in saying, " The glory of arms cannot compare with the
happiness of living in peace." He anticipated our defi-
nition of a republic, when he said " it was formed upon
the *equality of all the citizens*," — good words, not yet

practically verified in all our States. Such a government he, living under a monarchy, bravely pronounced
the best of all; but he added that he "had never known
a constitution truly republican." This was in 1778.
With similar plainness he announced that "the destruction of the Ottoman empire would be a real good for all
the nations of Europe," and, he added still further, for
humanity also, because it would involve the abolition of
negro slavery, and because to strip "our oppressors is
not to attack, but to vindicate, the common rights of
humanity." With such thoughts and aspirations, the
prophet died.

But I have no purpose of writing a biography, or even
a character. All that I intend is an introduction to
Turgot's prophetic words. When only twenty-three
years of age, while still an ecclesiastic at the Sorbonne,
the future minister delivered a discourse on the Progress
of the Human Mind, in which, after describing the commercial triumphs of the ancient Phœnicians, covering
the coasts of Greece and Asia with their colonies, he
lets drop these remarkable words : —

"Les colonies sont comme des fruits qui ne tiennent à
l'arbre que jusqu'à leur maturité ; devenues suffisantes à
elles-mêmes, elles firent ce que fit depuis Carthage, — *ce
que fera un jour l'Amérique.*" [1]

"Colonies are like fruits, which hold to the tree only until their maturity ; when sufficient for themselves, they did
that which Carthage afterwards did, — *that which some day
America will do.*"

On this most suggestive declaration, Dupont de Ne-

<hr/>

[1] Turgot, Œuvres, Tom. II. p. 66. See also Condorcet, Œuvres, Tom.
IV., Vie de Turgot ; Louis Blanc, Histoire de la Révolution Française, Tom.
I. pp. 527 – 533.

mours, the editor of Turgot's works, in 1808, remarks in a note : —

"It was in 1750 that M. Turgot, being then only twenty-three years old, and devoted in a seminary to the study of theology, divined, foresaw the revolution which has formed the United States, — which has detached them from the European power apparently the most capable of retaining its colonies under its domination."

At the time Turgot wrote, Canada was a French possession; but his words are as applicable to this colony as to the United States. When will the fruit be ripe?

In contrast with this precise prediction, and yet in harmony with it, are the words of Montesquieu, in his ingenious work, which saw the light in 1748, two years before the discourse of Turgot. In the famous chapter, "How the laws contribute to form the manners, customs, and character of a nation," we have a much-admired picture of a "free nation," — "inhabiting an island," — where, without naming England, it is easy to recognize her greatness and glory. And here we meet a Delphic passage, also without a name, pointing to the British Colonies : [1] —

"If this nation sent out colonies, it would do it more to extend its commerce than its empire.

"As people like to establish elsewhere what is found established at home, it would give to the people of its colonies its own form of government, and this government carrying with it prosperity, *we should see great peoples form themselves in the very forests which it sent them to inhabit.*"

The future greatness of the Colonies is insinuated

[1] De l'Esprit des Lois, Livre XIX. Chap. XXVII.

rather than foretold, and here the prophetic voice is silent. Nothing is said of the impending separation and the beginning of a new nation; so that plainly Montesquieu saw our future less than Turgot.

The youthful prophet did not lose his penetrating vision with years. In the same spirit and with immense vigor he wrote to the English philosopher, Josiah Tucker, September 17, 1770: —

"As a citizen of the world, I see with joy the approach of an event which, more than all the books of philosophers, will dissipate the phantom of commercial jealousy. *I mean the separation of your colonies from the mother country*, WHICH WILL BE FOLLOWED SOON BY THAT OF ALL AMERICA FROM EUROPE. It is then that the discovery of this part of the world will become to us truly useful. It is then that it will multiply our enjoyments much more abundantly than when we purchased them with torrents of blood. The English, the French, the Spaniards, will use sugar, coffee, indigo, and will sell their products precisely as the Swiss do to-day, and they will have also, as the Swiss people, the advantage that this sugar, this coffee, this indigo, will serve no longer as a pretext for intriguers to precipitate their nation into ruinous wars and to oppress them with taxes." [1]

It is impossible not to feel in this passage the sure grasp of our American destiny. How clearly and courageously he announces the inevitable future! But the French philosopher-statesman again took the tripod.

This was in the discharge of his duties as Minister of the Crown and in reply to a special application. His

[1] Œuvres (ed. Daire), Tom. II. p. 803.

noble opinion is dated 6th April, 1776. Its character
appears in a few sentences : —

"The present war will probably end in the absolute independence of the colonies, and that event will certainly be *the
epoch of the greatest revolution in the commerce and politics not
of England only, but of all Europe.* . . . . When the English
themselves shall recognize the independence of their colonies,
every mother country will be forced in like manner to exchange
its dominion over its colonies for bonds of friendship and fra-
ternity. . . . . When the *total separation of America* shall have
healed the European nations of the jealousy of commerce, there
will exist among men one great cause of war the less, and it
is very difficult not to desire an event which is to accomplish
this good for the human race." [1]

His letter to the English Dr. Price, on the American
Constitution, abounds in profound observations and in
prophecy. It was written just at the time when France
openly joined against England in our war of Independence, and is dated March 22, 1778,[2] but did not see the
light until 1784, some years after the death of the author, when it was published by Dr. Price.[3] Its criticism of the American constitutions aroused John Adams
to his elaborate work in their "Defence." [4]

Of our Union before the adoption of the National
Constitution he writes : —

"In the general union of the provinces among themselves
I do not see a coalition, a fusion of all the parts, making
but one body, one and homogeneous. It is nothing but an

[1] Bancroft, History of the United States, Vol. VIII. pp. 337, 338.
[2] Turgot, Œuvres (ed. Daire), Tom. II. 805 – 811.
[3] Observations on the Importance of the American Revolution, Appendix.
[4] Works, Vol. IV. 278 – 281, where is found the larger part of the letter of
Turgot.

aggregation of parts always too separated, and preserving
always a tendency to division, through the diversity of laws,
manners, opinions, — through the inequality of their actual
forces, — more also by the inequality of their ulterior progress. It is nothing but a copy of the Dutch Republic;
but this never had anything to fear as the American Republic from possible increase of some of its provinces. All
this edifice is supported down to this time on the false basis
of the very ancient and very vulgar politics, on the prejudice that nations and provinces can have interests, as
nations and provinces, different from those of individuals to
be free and to defend their property against brigands and
conquerors; a pretended interest to have more commerce
than others, not to buy merchandise abroad, to force foreigners to consume their productions and their manufactures; a pretended interest to have a vaster territory, to
acquire this or that province, this or that island, this or
that village; an interest to inspire fear in other nations;
interest to surpass them in the glory of arms, in that of arts
and sciences."

Among the evils to be overcome are, in the Southern
Colonies too great an inequality of fortunes, and especially the large number of black slaves, whose slavery
is incompatible with a good political constitution, and
who, even when restored to liberty, will cause embar-
rassment by forming two nations in the same State. In
all the Colonies he deprecates prejudice, attachment to
established forms, the preservation of certain taxes, the
fear of those which should be substituted, the vanity of
the Colonies who deem themselves most powerful, and
the wretched beginning of national pride. Happily he
adds: "I think the Americans forced to aggrandizement,
not by war, but by husbandry." And he then proceeds
to his aspirations : —

" It is impossible not to offer vows that this people may arrive at all the prosperity of which it is susceptible. It is the hope of the human race. It can become its model. It must prove to the world, by the fact, that men can be free and tranquil, and can dispense with the chains of all kinds which the tyrants and charlatans of every cloth have pretended to impose under the pretext of public good. It must give the example of political liberty, of religious liberty, of commercial and industrial liberty. The asylum which it opens to the oppressed of all nations must console the earth. The facility it affords for escape from a bad government will force the European governments to be just and enlightened. The rest of the world, little by little, will open their eyes to the nothingness of the illusions in which politicians have nursed them. To this end it is necessary that America should take guaranties, and should not become, as so many of your ministerial writers have repeated, an image of an Europe, *a heap of divided Powers*, disputing about territory or commercial profits, and continually cementing the slavery of people with their own blood."

After these admirable thoughts, so full of wisdom and prophecy, Turgot alludes to the impending war between France and England : —

" Our two nations are going to do each other reciprocally much evil, probably without either obtaining any real advantage. The increase of debts and liabilities and the ruin of a great many citizens will be, perhaps, the only result. England seems nearer to this than France. If instead of this war you had been able to act in good spirit from the first moment, — if it had been given to government to do in advance what infallibly it will be forced to do later, — if national opinion had permitted your government to anticipate events, — and, supposing that it had foreseen them, it had been able to consent at once to the Independence of

America without making war on anybody, — I am firmly
convinced that your nation would have lost nothing by
the change. It will lose now what it has already expended,
and what it shall expend besides. It will experience for
some time a great falling off in its commerce, great domestic
disturbances, if it is forced to bankruptcy, and, whatever
may arrive, a great diminution in its influence abroad.
But this last matter is of small importance in the real happiness of a people. I do not think it can make you become
a contemptible nation, and throw you into slavery.

"Your present troubles, your future happiness, will be attributed to a necessary amputation, which is, perhaps, the
only means of saving you from the gangrene of luxury and
corruption. If in your agitations you could correct your
Constitution by rendering elections annual, by apportioning
the right of representation so that it shall be more equal
and more proportioned to the interests of those represented,
you would gain from this revolution as much, perhaps, as
America; for your liberty would remain, and with this and
by this your other losses would repair themselves."

Reading such words, the heart throbs and the pulse
beats. Government inspired by such a spirit would become divine, nations would live at peace together, and
people everywhere be happy.

HORACE WALPOLE, 1754, 1777, 1779.

MOST unlike Turgot in character, but with something
of the same spirit of prophecy, and associated in time,
was Horace Walpole, youngest son of England's remarkable Prime Minister, Sir Robert Walpole. With
the former life was serious always, and human improvement the perpetual passion; with the latter there was

a constant desire for amusement, and the world was little more than a curious gimcrack.

Horace Walpole was born 5th October, 1717, and died 2d March, 1797, being at his death Earl of Orford. According to his birth he was a man of fashion; for a time a member of Parliament; a man of letters always. To his various talents he added an aggregation of miscellaneous tastes, of which his house at Strawberry Hill was an illustration, — being an elegant "Old Curiosity Shop," with pictures, books, manuscripts, prints, armor, china, historic relics, and art in all its forms, which he had collected at no small outlay of time and money. Though aristocratic in life, he boasted that his principles were not monarchical. On the two sides of his bed were hung engravings of Magna Charta and of the Sentence of Charles I., the latter with the inscription *Major* Charta. Sleeping between two such memorials, he might be suspected of sympathy with America, although the aristocrat was never absent. His Memoirs, Journals, Anecdotes of Painters in England, and other works, are less famous than his multifarious correspondence, which is the best in English literature, and, according to French judgment, nearer than any other of our language to that of Madame de Sévigné, whom he never wearied in praising. It is free, easy, gossipy, historic, and spicy.

But I deal with him now only as a prophet. And I begin with his "Memoirs of the last Ten Years of the Reign of George II.," where we find the record that the Colonists were seeking independence. This occurs in his description of the Duke of Newcastle as Secretary of State for the Colonies, during the long Walpole administration. Illustrating what he calls the Duke's "mercurial inattention," he says: "It would not be credited what reams of papers, representations, memorials, petitions from that quarter of the world [the Colonies], lay mouldering and unopened in his office"; and then, showing his ignorance, he narrates how, when it was hinted that there should be some defence for Annapolis, he replied with evasive, lisping hurry: "Annapolis, Annapolis! O yes, Annapolis must be defended, — to be sure, Annapolis should be defended; — where is Annapolis?" But this negligence did not prevent him from exalting the prerogative of the crown; and here the author says: —

"The instructions to Sir Danvers Osborn, a new governor of New York, seemed better calculated for the latitude of Mexico and for a Spanish tribunal than for a free, rich British settlement, and in such opulence and of such haughtiness, that *suspicions had long been conceived of their meditating to throw off their dependence on their mother country.*"

This stands in the Memoirs under date of March, 1754, where the editor in a note remarks, "If, as the author asserts, this was written at the time, it is a very remarkable passage."[1]   By the will of the author the book was "to be kept unopened and unsealed" until a certain person named should attain the age of twenty-five years.   It was published in 1822.   Perhaps the honesty of this entry will be better appreciated when it is noted that, only a few pages later,[2] Washington, whom the author afterwards admired, is spoken of as "this brave braggart," who "learned to blush for his rhodomontade."

[1] Vol. I. p. 344.
[2] Page 347. See also Letter to Horace Mann, 6th October, 1754. **Letters** by Cunningham, Vol. II. p. 398.

As the difficulties with the Colonies increased, he became more sympathetic and prophetic. In a letter to Horace Mann, 24th February, 1774, he wrote : —

"We have no news, public or private; but there is an ostrich-egg laid in America, where the Bostonians have canted three hundred chests of tea into the ocean ; for they will not drink tea with our Parliament. . . . . Lord Chatham talked of conquering America in Germany. *I believe England will be conquered some day in New England or Bengal.*"

In May, 1774, his sympathies again appear : —

"Nothing was more shocking than the king's laughing and saying at his levee *that he had as lief fight the Bos- tonians as the French.* It was only to be paralleled by James II. sporting on Jeffries's campaign in the West." [1]

And, under date of 28th May, 1775, we have his record of the encounter at Lexington, with the reflec- tion : —

"Thus was the civil war begun and a victory, the first fruits of it on the side of the Americans, whom Lord Sand- wich had had the folly and rashness to proclaim cowards." [2]

. His letters to the Countess of Ossory, written during the war, show his irrepressible sentiments. Thus under date of 9th November, 1775 : —

"I think this country undone almost beyond redemption. Victory in any war but a civil one fascinates mankind with a vision of glory. What should we gain by triumph itself? Would America laid waste, deluged with blood, plundered,

---

[1] Journal of the Reign of King George III. from 1771 to 1783, edited by Doran, Vol. I. p. 366.
[2] Ibid., p. 491.

enslaved, replace America flourishing, rich, and free? Do
we want to reign over it, as the Spaniards over Peru, de-
populated? Are desolate regions preferable to commercial
cities?" [1]

Then under date of 6th July, 1777 : —

"My humble opinion is, that we shall never recover
America and that France will take care that we shall never
recover ourselves." [2]

"Friday night late," 5th December, 1777, he breaks
forth : —

"Send for Lord Chatham! they had better send for
General Washington, madam, — or at least for our troops
back. . . . . No, madam, we do not want ministers that
would protract our difficulties. I look on them but as
beginning now, and am far from thinking that there is any
man or set of men able enough to extricate us. *I own there
are very able Englishmen left, but they happen to be on t'other
side of the Atlantic.* If his Majesty hopes to find them here,
I doubt he will be mistaken." [3]

"Thursday night," 11th December, 1777, his feelings
overflow in no common language : —

"Was ever proud insolent nation sunk so low? Burke
and Charles Fox told him [Lord North] the Administration
thought of nothing but keeping their places ; and so they
will, and the members their pensions, and the nation its
infamy. Were I Franklin, I would order the Cabinet
Council to come to me at Paris with ropes about their
necks, and then kick them back ·to St. James's.

[1] Vol. I. p 200: Letter LXXIV.
[2] Ibid., p. 278: Letter CVI.
[3] Ibid., pp. 315, 316: Letter CXX.

" Well, madam, as I told Lord Ossory t'other day, I am satisfied. *Old England is safe, that is, America, whither the true English retired under Charles I.* This is Nova Scotia, and I care not what becomes of it. . . . . Adieu, madam ! I am at last not sorry you have no son, and your daughters, I hope, will be married to Americans, and not in this dirty, despicable island." [1]

All this is elevated by his letter of 17th February, 1779, where he says : —

" Liberty has still a continent to exist in. I do not care a straw who is minister in this abandoned country. It is the *good old cause of freedom* that I have at heart." [2]

Thus with constancy, where original principle was doubtless quickened by party animosity, did Horace Walpole maintain the American cause and predict a new home for Liberty.

JOHN ADAMS, 1755, 1765, 1776, 1780, 1783, 1785, 1813.

NEXT in time among the prophets was John Adams, who has left on record at different dates predictions showing a second-sight of no common order. Of his life I need say nothing, except that he was born 19th October, 1735, and died 4th July, 1826. I mention the predictions in the order of utterance.

1. While teaching a school at Worcester, and when under twenty years of age, he wrote a letter to one of his youthful companions, bearing date 12th October, 1755, which is a marvel of foresight. Fifty-two years afterwards, when already much of its prophecy had been

---

[1] Vol. I. pp. 318, 319: Letter CXXI.
[2] Ibid., p. 337: Letter CXXIX.

fulfilled, the original was returned to its author by the son of his early comrade and correspondent, Nathan Webb, who was at the time dead. After remarking gravely on the rise and fall of nations, with illustrations from Carthage and Rome, he proceeds : —

" England began to increase in power and magnificence, and is now the greatest nation of the globe. Soon after the Reformation, a few people came over into this New World for conscience' sake. Perhaps this apparently trivial incident *may transfer the great seat of empire to America. It looks likely to me ;* for if we can remove the turbulent Gallics, our people, according to the exactest computations, will, in another century, become more numerous than England itself. Should this be the case, since we have, I may say, all the naval stores of the nations in our hands, it will be easy to obtain the mastery of the seas ; and then the united force of all Europe will not be able to subdue us. The only way to keep us from setting up for ourselves is to disunite us. *Divide et impera.* Keep us in distinct colonies, and then, some great men in each colony desiring the monarchy of the whole, they will destroy each other's influence, and keep the country *in equilibrio.*" [1]

On this his son, John Quincy Adams, famous for important service and high office, remarks : —

" Had the political part of it been written by the minister of state of a European monarchy, at the close of a long life spent in the government of nations, it would have been pronounced worthy of the united wisdom of a Burleigh, a Sully, or an Oxenstiern. . . . . *In one bold outline he has exhibited by anticipation a long succession of prophetic history, the fulfilment of which is barely yet in progress, responding*

[1] Works, Vol. I. p. 23. See also Vol. IX. pp. 591, 592.

exactly hitherto to his foresight, but the full accomplishment of which is reserved for the development of after ages. The extinction of the power of France in America, the union of the British North American Colonies, the achievement of their independence, and the establishment of their ascendency in the community of civilized nations by the means of their naval power, are all foreshadowed in this letter, with a clearness of perception and a distinctness of delineation which time has done little more than to convert into historical fact." [1]

2. Another beautiful instance followed ten years later. In the beginning of 1765, Jeremy Gridley, the eminent lawyer of colonial days, formed a law club or sodality at Boston, for the mutual improvement of its members. Here John Adams produced the original sketch of his "Dissertation on the Canon and Feudal Law," which appeared in the "Boston Gazette" of August, 1768, was reprinted in London about 1782, and in Philadelphia in 1783.[2] The sketch began : —

"This sodality has given rise to the following speculation of my own, which I commit to writing as hints for future inquiries rather than as a satisfactory theory." [3]

In this dissertation, the writer dwells especially upon the settlers of British America, of whom he says : —

"After their arrival here, they began their settlement and formed their plan both of ecclesiastical and civil governments in direct opposition to the canon and federal systems." [4]

This excellent statement was followed in the original

1 Works, Vol. I. pp. 24, 25.   3 Ibid., Vol. I. pp. 65, 66.
2 Ibid., Vol. III. p. 447.   4 Ibid., Vol. III. p. 451.

sketch, communicated to the sodality, by this passage, which does not appear in the printed dissertation : —

"I always consider the settlement of America with reverence, as the opening of a grand scene and design in Providence for the illumination of the ignorant and the emancipation of the slavish part of mankind all over the earth." [1]

On these prophetic words, his son, John Quincy Adams, remarks : —

"This sentence was perhaps omitted from an impression that it might be thought to savor not merely of enthusiasm but of extravagance. Who would now deny that this magnificent anticipation had been already to a great degree realized? Who does not now see that the accomplishment of this great object is already placed beyond all possibility of failure?" [2]

His grandson, Charles Francis Adams, alluding to the changes which took place in the original sketch, says : —

"As not infrequently happens, however, in this process, one stray passage was lost by it, which at this time must be regarded as the most deserving of any to be remembered." [3]

Thus again, at an early day, did this prophet discern the future. How true it is that the mission of this Republic is " the illumination of the ignorant," and still further "the emancipation of the slavish part of mankind all over the earth." Universal enlightenment and universal emancipation ! And the first great stage was National Independence.

---

[1] Works, Vol. I. p. 66; Vol. III. p. 452.   [3] Ibid., Vol. III. p. 448.
[2] Ibid., Vol. I. p. 66.

3. The Declaration of Independence bears date 4th July, 1776, for on that day it was signed; but the vote which determined it was on the 2d July. On the 3d July, John Adams, in a letter to his wife, wrote : —

" Yesterday the greatest question was decided which ever was debated in America, and a greater, perhaps, never was nor will be decided among men. . . . . I am surprised at the suddenness as well as greatness of this revolution. Britain has been filled with folly, and America with wisdom. At least this is my judgment. Time must determine. *It is the will of Heaven that the two countries should be sundered forever.* . . . . The day is past. The second day of July, 1776, will be the most memorable epocha in the history of America. *I am apt to believe that it will be celebrated by succeeding generations as the great anniversary festival.* It ought to be commemorated, as the day of deliverance, by solemn acts of devotion to God Almighty. It ought to be solemnized with pomp and parade, with shows, games, sports, guns, bells, bonfires, and illuminations, from one end of this continent to the other, from this time forward, forevermore. You will think me transported with enthusiasm, but I am not. I am well aware of the toil and blood and treasure that it will cost us to maintain this Declaration, and support and defend these States. *Yet, through all the gloom, I can see the ray of ravishing light and glory ; and that posterity will triumph in that day's transaction,* even although we should rue it, which I trust in God we shall not." [1]

Here is a comprehensive prophecy, first, that the two countries would be separated forever ; secondly, that the anniversary of Independence would be celebrated as a great annual festival ; and, thirdly, that posterity would triumph in this transaction, where, through all

1 Works, Vol. I. pp. 230, 232.

the gloom, shone rays of ravishing light and glory, — all of which has been fulfilled to the letter. Recent events give to the Declaration additional importance. For a long time its great promises that all men are equal, and that rightful government stands only on the consent of the governed, were disowned by our country. Now that at last they are beginning to prevail, there is increased reason to celebrate the day on which the mighty Declaration was made, and new occasion for triumph in the rays of ravishing light and glory.

4. Here is another prophetic passage in a letter dated at Paris, 13th July, 1780, and addressed to the Count de Vergennes of France, pleading the cause of the colonists : —

"The United States of America are a great and powerful people, whatever European statesmen may think of them. If we take into our estimate the numbers and the character of her people, the extent, variety, and fertility of her soil, her commerce, and her skill and materials for shipbuilding, and her seamen, excepting France, Spain, England, Germany, and Russia, there is not a state in Europe so powerful. Breaking off such a nation as this from the English so suddenly, and uniting it so closely with France, is one of the most extraordinary events that ever happened among mankind." [1]

Perhaps this may be considered statement rather than prophecy ; but it illustrates the prophetic character of the writer.

5. While at Amsterdam, in 1780, Mr. Adams met a gentleman whom he calls "the giant of the law," Mr. Calkoen. After an unsatisfactory attempt at conversation, where neither spoke the language of the other, it

[1] Works, Vol. VII. p. 527.

was arranged that the latter should propound a series
of questions in writing, which the American minister
undertook to answer. The questions were in Dutch,
the answers in English. Among the questions was
this : "Whether America in and of itself, by means of
purchasing or exchanging the productions of the several provinces, would be.able to continue the war for
six, eight, or ten years, even if they were entirely de-
prived of the trade with Europe, or their allies, ex-
hausted by the war and forced to make a separate
peace, were to leave them?" To this question our
prophet replied : —

"This is an extreme case. . . . . Why, then, should we
put cases that we know can never happen? However, I can
inform you that the case was often put before the war broke
out; and I have heard the common farmers in America
reasoning upon these cases seven years ago. I have heard
them say, if Great Britain could build a wall of brass a
thousand feet high all along the sea-coast, at low-water
mark, we can live and be happy. *America is most undoubtedly capable of being the most independent country upon earth.*
It produces everything for the necessity, comfort, and con-
venience of life, and many of the luxuries too. So that if
there were an eternal separation between Europe and America, the inhabitants of America would not only live but
multiply, and, for what I know, be wiser, better, and happier than they will be as it is."[1]

Here is an assertion of conditions essential to independence over "the most independent country upon
earth," with a promise that "the inhabitants will
multiply."

[1] Works, Vol. VII. p. 275. Twenty-six Letters upon Interesting Subjects respecting the Revolution of America, written in Holland in the year
MDCCLXX.

3 *

6. In an official letter to the President of Congress, dated at Amsterdam, 5th September, 1780, the same writer, while proposing an American Academy for refining, improving, and ascertaining the English language, predicts the extension of this language : —

"*English is destined to be in the next and succeeding centuries more generally the language of the world than Latin was in the last or French is in the present age.* The reason of this is obvious, — because the increasing population in America, and their universal connection and correspondence with all nations, will, aided by the influence of England in the world, whether great or small, force their language into general use, in spite of all the obstacles that may be thrown in their way, if any such there should be." [1]

In another letter of unofficial character, dated at Amsterdam, 23d September, 1780, he thus repeats his prophecy : —

"You must know *I have undertaken to prophesy that English will be the most respectable language in the world, and the most universally read and spoken in the next century, if not before the close of this.* American population will in the next age produce a greater number of persons who will speak English than any other language, and these persons will have more general acquaintance and conversation with all other nations than any other people." [2]

David Hume in a letter to Gibbon, 24th October, 1767, had already written : —

"Our solid and increasing establishments in America, where we need less dread the inundation of barbarians, *promise a superior stability and duration to the English language.*" [3]

[1] Works, Vol. VII. p. 250.   [2] Ibid., Vol. IX. p. 510.
[3] Gibbon, Memoirs, Chap. VII., Notes and Additions.

But these more moderate words which did credit to the discernment of the philosopher-historian were then unpublished.

The prophecy of John Adams is already accomplished. Of all the European languages, English is most extensively spoken. Through England and the United States it has become the language of commerce, which, sooner or later, must embrace the globe. The German philologist, Grimm, has followed our American prophet in saying that it "seems chosen, like its people, to rule in future times in a still greater degree in all the corners of the earth."[1]

Another field was opened by a European correspondent, John Luzac, who writes from Leyden, under date of 14th September, 1780, that, in pleading the cause of American Independence, he has twenty times encountered, from sensible and educated people, an objection which he sets forth in French as follows: —

"Yes, but if America becomes free, she will some day give the law to Europe. She will take away our islands, and our colonies at Guiana; she will seize all the Antilles; she will engulf Mexico, even Peru, Chili, and Brazil; she will appropriate our freighting commerce; she will pay her benefactors with ingratitude."[2]

To this Mr. Adams replied, in a letter from Amsterdam, 15th September, 1780: —

"I have met often in Europe with the same species of reasoners that you describe; but I find they are not numerous. Among men of reflection the sentiment is generally different, and that no power in Europe has anything to fear from America. The principal interest of

[1] Keith Johnston, Physical Atlas, p. 114.
[2] Works, Vol. VIII. p. 254.

America for many centuries to come will be landed, and
her chief occupation agriculture. Manufactures and commerce will be but secondary objects and always subservient
to the other. America will be the country to produce raw
materials for manufacture; but Europe will be the country
of manufactures, and the commerce of America can never
increase but in a certain proportion to the growth of its
agriculture, until its whole territory is filled up with in
habitants, which will not be in some hundreds of years."

After enumerating tar, iron, and timber as American
articles, he says: —

"In fact, the Atlantic is so long and difficult a navigation,
that the Americans will never be able to afford to carry
to the European market great quantities of these articles."

If the prophet fails here, he is none the less wise
in the suggestion with which he closes: —

"If Europe cannot prevent, or, rather, if any particular
nation of Europe cannot prevent, the independence of
America, then the sooner her independence is acknowledged the better; the less likely she will be to become
warlike, enterprising, and ambitious. The truth is, however, that America can never unite in any war but a
defensive one."[1]

Had the prophet foreseen the increasing facilities
of commerce, the triumphs of steam, the floating masses
of transportation, the wonders of navigation, quickened
and guided by the telegraph, and to these had he added
the diversified industry of the country, extending, ex-
panding, and prevailing, his remarkable vision, which
already saw so much, would have viewed other glories
in assured certainty.

[1] Works, Vol. VII. p. 256.

8. There is another prophecy, at once definite and broad, from the same eminent quarter. In a letter dated London, 17th October, 1785, and addressed to John Jay, at the time Secretary for Foreign Affairs under the Confederation, John Adams reveals his conviction of the importance of France to us, "while England held a province in America";[1] and then, in another letter, dated 21st October, 1785, reports the saying of people about him, "*that Canada and Nova Scotia must soon be ours;* there must be war for it; they know how it will end, but the sooner the better. This done, we shall be forever at peace; till then, never."[2] These intimations foreshadow the prophecy found in the Preface to his "Defence of the American Constitutions," written in London, while Minister there, and dated Grosvenor Square, 1st January, 1787 : —

"The United States of America have exhibited, perhaps, the first example of governments erected on the simple principles* of nature. . . . . Thirteen governments thus founded on the natural authority of the people alone, without a pretence of miracle or mystery, and *which are destined to spread over the northern part of that whole quarter of the globe,* are a great point gained in favor of the rights of mankind. The experiment is made, and has completely succeeded."[3]

Here is foretold nothing less than that our system of government is to embrace the whole continent of North America.

9. This series may be concluded by other words, general in character, but deeply prophetic, showing a con-

---

[1] Works, Vol. VIII. p. 322.
[2] Ibid. p. 33.
[3] Ibid., Vol. IV. p. 293.

stant sense of the unfolding grandeur and influence of
the Republic.

The first is from the concluding chapter of the work
last cited, and in harmony with the Preface : —

"A prospect into futurity in America is like contemplating the heavens through the telescopes of Herschel.
Objects stupendous in their magnitudes and motions strike
us from all quarters and fill us with amazement." [1]

Thus, also, he writes to Thomas Jefferson, November
15, 1813 : —

" Many hundred years must roll away before we shall be
corrupted. *Our pure, virtuous, public-spirited, federative republic will last forever, govern the globe, and introduce the perfection of man.*" [2]

Then, again, in a letter to H. Niles, 13th February,
1818 : —

" The American Revolution was not a common event.
Its effects and consequences have already been awful over
a great part of the globe. *And when and where are they
to cease ?*" [3]

The prophetic spirit which filled the "visions" of
youth continued in the "dreams" of age. Especially
was he constant in foreseeing the widening reach of
the great Revolution he had helped at its beginning;
and this arrested the attention of his eloquent eulogist
at Faneuil Hall.[4]

---

[1] Works, Vol. VI. p. 218.
[2] Complete Works of Jefferson, Vol. VI. p. 258.
[3] Works, Vol X. p. 282.
[4] Daniel Webster's Discourse in commemoration of the Lives and Services of John Adams and Thomas Jefferson, delivered in Faneuil Hall,
Boston, August 2, 1826: Works, Vol. I. p. 139.

MARQUIS DE MONTCALM, 1758, 1759.

IF I enter the name of the Marquis de Montcalm on this list, it is because prophetic words have been attributed to him, which at different periods have attracted no small attention. He was born near Nismes in France, 1712, and died at Quebec, 13th September, 1759, being at the time commander of the French forces in Canada. As a soldier he was the peer of his opponent, Wolfe, who perished in the same battle, and they have since enjoyed a common fame.

In 1777, amidst the heats of our Revolutionary contest, a publication was put forth by Almon, the pamphleteer, in French and English on opposite pages, entitled " Letters from the Marquis de Montcalm, Governor-General of Canada in the years 1757, 1758, and 1759," and the soldier reappeared as prophet.

The first letter is addressed to M. de Berryer, First Commissioner of the Marine of France, and purports to be dated at Montreal, 4th April, 1757. It contains the copy of an elaborate communication from "S. J." of Boston, proposing a scheme for undermining the power of Great Britain in the Colonies, by free trade with France through Canada, and predicting that " all our colonies in less than ten years will catch fire."[1] In transmitting this letter Montcalm did little more than indorse its sentiments ; but in his second letter to the same person, dated at Montreal, 1st October, 1758, he says : —

" All these informations which I every day receive confirm me in my opinion that *England will one day lose her colonies on the continent of America ;* and if Canada should then be in the hands of an able governor who understands

[1] Page 8.

his business, he will have a thousand opportunities of hastening the event ; this is the only advantage we can reap of all it has cost us."[1]

In the third letter, addressed to M. Molé, First President of the Parliament of Paris, and dated at the camp before Quebec, 24th August, 1759, on the eve of the fatal battle in which both commanders fell, Montcalm mounts the tripod : —

"They are in a condition to give us battle, which I must not refuse, and which I cannot hope to gain. . . . . The event must decide. But of one thing be certain, that I probably shall not survive the loss of the colony.[2] . . . . I shall at least console myself in my defeat and on the loss of the colony, by the full persuasion that this defeat will one day serve my country more than a victory, and that the conqueror, in aggrandizing himself, will find his tomb in the country he gains from us.[3] . . . . All the English colonies would long since have shaken off the yoke, each province would have formed itself into a little independent republic, if the fear of seeing the French at their door had not been a check upon them.[4] . . . . Canada, once taken by the English, would in a few years suffer much more from being forced to be English. . . . . They would soon be of no use to England, and perhaps they would oppose her."[5]

At once on their appearance these letters played an important part in the "high life" of politics. The "Monthly Review"[6] called them "genuine." The "Gentleman's Magazine"[7] said that "the sagacity of this accomplished general was equal to his bravery," and quoted what it characterized as a "remarkable prediction." In the House of Lords, 30th May, 1777, dur-

[1] Page 18.   [3] Page 22.   [5] Page 27.   [7] July, 1777, p. 342.
[2] Page 21.   [4] Page 24.   [6] April, 1777, p. 306.

ing a debate begun by Lord Chatham, and flashing with great names, Lord Shelburne said that "they had been discovered to be a forgery";[1] but Lord Mansfield, the illustrious Chief Justice, relied upon the letters, "which he insisted were not spurious."[2] In another important debate in the House of Lords, 5th March, 1778, Earl Temple, after quoting Montcalm, "observed that the authenticity of these letters had been often disputed; but he could affirm that he saw them in manuscript among the papers of a minister now deceased, long before they made their appearance in print, and at a time when American independence was in the contemplation of a very few persons indeed."[3] Such was the contemporary testimony; but the pamphlet shared the fate of the numerous brood engendered by the war.

Oblivion seemed to have settled on these letters, when their republication at Gibraltar, as late as 1858, by an author who treated them as genuine,[4] attracted the attention of Thomas Carlyle, who proceeded to make them famous again, by introducing them as an episode in his Life of Frederick, sometimes called the Great. Montcalm appears once more as prophet, and the readers of the career of the Prussian monarch turn with wonder to the inspired Frenchman, with "his power of faithful observation, his sagacity and talent of prophecy so considerable."[5] Then, quoting a considerable portion of the last letter, the great author exclaims at different points: "Prediction first"; "This is a curi-

[1] Parliamentary History, Vol. IX. p. 346.
[2] Ibid., p. 351.
[3] Ibid., p. 847.
[4] The Plains of Abraham, Notes original and selected, by Lieutenant-Colonel Beathon.
[5] History of Frederick II. of Prussia, Vol. V. p. 557 (London, 1865).

ously exact prediction "; " Prediction second, which is still more curious."[1]

If the letter quoted by Carlyle were genuine, as he accepted it (also as was evidently accepted by Lord John Russell[2]), and as the family of Montcalm seem to believe, it would indicate for the soldier all that was claimed by his descendant when, after speaking of his " political foresight," he added that it " was proved by one of his letters, in which he made a remarkable prophecy concerning the American Revolution."[3]   Certainly, — if the letter is not an invention; but such is the present impression.   On the title-page of the original pamphlet, in the Library of Harvard University, Sparks, whose judgment is of great weight, has written: " These letters are unquestionably spurious."   Others unite with him.   It is impossible to read the paper in the " Proceedings of the Massachusetts Historical Society," already quoted, and the pungent note of George Stevens, in his catalogue entitled *Bibliotheca Historica*, under the title of the much debated pamphlet, without feeling that whatever may have been the merits of Montcalm as a soldier, his title as a prophet cannot be accepted.   His name is introduced here that I may not omit an instance which has attracted attention in more than one generation.

THE DUKE DE CHOISEUL, 1767, 1768.

ANOTHER Frenchman in this far-sighted list was the Count de Stainville, afterwards Duke de Choiseul,

---

[1] History of Frederick II. of Prussia, Vol. V. p. 558.

[2] House of Commons, 8th February, 1850. Hanford, Parliamentary Debates, Third Series, Vol. CVIII. p. 537.

[3] Remarks of Mr. Parkman. Proceedings of the Massachusetts Historical Society, 1869 – 70, p. 113.

born 28th June, 1719, and died May, 1785. His brilliant career as diplomatist and statesman was preceded by a career of arms with rapid promotion, so that at the age of forty he became lieutenant-general. Meanwhile he was ambassador at Rome and then at Vienna, being the two pinnacles of diplomatic life. In 1758 he became Minister of Foreign Affairs, also duke and peer; then Minister of War; but in 1766 he resumed the Foreign Office, which he held till 1770, when he was disgraced. The king could not pardon the contempt with which, although happy in the smiles of Madame de Pompadour, the Prime Minister rejected the advances of her successor, the ignoble Du Barry; and he was exiled from court to live in his château on the Loire, where, dispensing a magnificent hospitality, he. was consoled by a loving wife and devoted friends.

He had charm of manner rather than person, with a genius for statesmanship recognized and commemorated in contemporary writings. Madame du Deffant speaks of him often in her correspondence, and depicts him in her circle when Franklin was first presented there. Horace Walpole returns to him in letters and in his memoirs, attributing to him "great parts," [1] calling him "daring and dashing, whose good-nature would not have checked his ambition from doing any splendid mischief." The Abbé Barthélemy, in his "Travels of Anacharsis," portrays him under the character of Arsane. Frederick of Prussia, so often called the Great, hailed him "coachman of Europe." And our own historian Bancroft does not hesitate to

---

[1] Letter to Countess of Ossory, 8th November, 1789. Letters by Cunningham, Vol. I. p. 234.

call him "the greatest minister of France since Richelieu."

The two volumes of memoirs purporting to be written
by himself and printed under his eyes in his cabinet
in 1778, were accidental pieces, written, but never collected by him, nor intended as memoirs.[1] In the
French treasure-house of these productions they are
of little value, if not unworthy of his fame.

Besides a brilliant and famous administration of
affairs, are several acts not to be forgotten. At Rome
his skill was shown in bringing Benedict XIV. to a common understanding on the bull *Unigenitus*. Through
him in 1764 the Jesuits were suppressed in France,
or were permitted only on condition of mingling with
the secular clergy. But nothing in his career was more
memorable than his foresight and courage with regard
to the English colonies. American Independence was
foreseen and helped by him.

The memoirs of Choiseul have little of the elevation
recognized in his statesmanship, nor are they anywhere
prophetic. Elsewhere his better genius was manifest,
especially in his diplomacy. This was recognized by
Talleyrand, who, in a paper on the advantages of new
colonies, read before the Institute towards the close
of the last century, characterized him as "one of the
men of our age who had the most of foresight in his
intelligence, *who already in* 1769 *foresaw the separation
of America from England*, and dreaded the partition
of Poland";[2] and he adds that "from this epoch he

---

[1] Mémoires de M. le Duc de Choiseul écrits par lui-même et imprimés
sous ses yeux dans son cabinet à Chanteloup en 1778. 2 livres, Chanteloup
et Paris, 1790.

[2] Essai sur les avantages à retirer des colonies dans les circonstances
présentes, par le citoyen Talleyrand, lu à l'Institut National, 25 Messidor.

sought by negotiations to prepare the cession of Egypt to France, that on the day the American colonies should escape, he might be ready with a substitute in the same productions and a more extended commerce."

Bancroft, whose work shows unprecedented access to original documents, recognizes the prevision of the French minister at an earlier date, as attested by the archives of the *French Foreign Office.* In 1764 he received the report of a special agent who had visited America. In 1767 he sent Baron de Kalb, afterwards an officer in our Revolution, — sparing no means to obtain information, and drawing even from New England sermons, of which curious extracts are preserved among the State Papers of France. In August of this year, writing to his plenipotentiary at London, the Minister says with regard to England and her colonies : " Let her but attempt to establish taxes in them, and those countries, greater than England in extent and perhaps becoming more populous, having fisheries, forests, shipping, corn, iron, and the like, will easily and fearlessly separate themselves from the mother country." [1] In the next year Du Chatelet, son of her who was the companion of Voltaire and the French translator of Newton, becomes his most sympathetic representative. To him the Minister wrote 15th July, 1768 : " According to the prognostications of sensible men, who have had an opportunity to study the character of the Americans and to measure their progress from day to day in the spirit of independence, this separation of the American Colonies from the metropolis sooner or

an V.   See Historical Characters by Sir Henry Lytton Bulwer, Vol. I. p. 461, Appendix

[1] Bancroft, History of the United States, Vol. VI. pp. 95, 96.

later must come.[1] .... I see all these difficulties,
and do not dissemble their extent; but I see also the
controlling interest of the Americans to profit by the
opportunity of a rupture to establish their independence."[2] Again he wrote, 22d November, 1768:
"The Americans will not lose out of their view their
rights and their privileges, and next to fanaticism for
religion, the fanaticism for liberty is the most daring
in its measures and the most dangerous in its consequences." That the plenipotentiary was not less
prompt in forecast appears in a letter of 9th November,
1768: "Without exaggerating the projects or the union
of the Colonies the time of their independence is very
near. .... Three years ago the separation of the English Colonies was looked upon as an object of attention
for the next generation; the germs were observed, but
no one could foresee that they would be so speedily
developed. This new order of things, this event which
will necessarily have the greatest influence on the
whole political system of Europe, will probably be
brought about within a very few years."[3] The Minister replied, 20th December, 1768: "Your views are
as subtle as they are comprehensive and well considered. The king is perfectly aware of their sagacity
and solidity, and I will communicate them to the
Court of Madrid."[4]

These passages show a persistency of view, which became the foundation of French policy, so that the Duke
was not merely a prophet but a practical statesman,
guided by remarkable foresight. He lived long enough
to witness the National Independence he had foretold,

---

[1] Bancroft, History of the United States, Vol. VI. p. 169.
[2] Ibid., p. 170.   [3] Ibid., p. 244.   [4] Ibid., p. 245.

and to meet Franklin at Paris, while saved from witnessing the overthrow of the monarchy he had served and the bloody harvest of the executioner, where a beloved sister was among the victims.

ABBÉ RAYNAL, 1770.

GUILLAUME THOMAS RAYNAL, of France, was born 11th March, 1711, and died 6th March, 1796, thus spanning, with his long life, from the failing years of Louis XIV. to the Reign of Terror, and embracing the prolonged period of intellectual activity which prepared the Revolution. Among contemporary "philosophers" his place was considerable. But he was a philosopher, with a cross of the adventurer and charlatan.

Beginning as Jesuit and as priest, he somewhat tardily escaped the constraints of the latter to employ the education of the former in literary enterprise. A long list of acknowledged works attests the activity of his pen, while others were attributed to him. With these avocations, yielding money, mingled jobbing and speculation, where even the slave-trade, afterwards furiously condemned, became a minister of fortune. In the bright and audacious circles of Paris, especially with Diderot and D'Holbach, he found society. The remarkable fame which he reached during life has ceased, and his voluminous writings slumber in oblivion, except, perhaps, a single one, which for a while played a great part and, by its prophetic spirit, vindicates a place in our American gallery.

Only the superficial character of this work appears in its title, — "Philosophical and Political History of the Establishments and of the Commerce of Europeans in

the two Indies," [1] being in four volumes. It was a frame
for pictures and declamations where freedom of thought
was practically illustrated. Therefore it was published
without the name of the author and at Amsterdam. This
was as early as 1770. Edition followed edition. The
Biographic Universelle reports no less than twenty regu-
lar and more than fifty pirated. At least four editions
of an English translation saw the light. It was translated, abridged, and reprinted in nearly all the languages
of Europe. The subject was interesting at the time,
but the peculiar treatment and the open assault upon
existing order gave the work zest and popularity.
Though often vicious in style, it was above the author in
force and character, so that it was easy to believe that
important parts were contributed by others. Diderot,
who passed his life in helping others, is said to have
supplied nearly a third of the whole. The work at last
drew down untimely vengeance. Inspired by its signal
success, the author, in 1780, after the lapse of a decade,
put forth an enlarged edition, with frontispiece and
portrait, the whole reënforced with insertions and additions, where Christianity and even the existence of a
God were treated with the license already applied to
other things. The Parliament of Paris, by a decree
dated May 21, 1781, handed the work to the public
executioner to be burned, and condemned the author
in person and goods Several years of exile followed.

The Revolution in France found the Abbé Raynal
mellowed by time, and with his sustaining philosophers
all dead. Declining active participation in the great
conflict, he reappeared at last, so far as to address the

---

*[1] Histoire Philosophique et Politique des Établissemens et du Commerce
des Européens dans les deux Indes.

President of the National Assembly a letter where he pleaded for moderation and an active government. The ancient assailant of kings now called for "the tutelary protection of the royal authority." The early *cant* was exchanged for *recant*.

The concluding book of the last edition of his famous work contains a chapter entitled "Has the Discovery of America been hurtful or useful to the Human Race?" And this same question he presented as the subject for a prize of twelve hundred francs to be awarded by the Academy of Lyons. Such a question reveals a strange confusion, inconsistent with all our prophetic voices, but to be pardoned at a time when the course of civilization was so little understood, and Buffon had announced, as the conclusion of science, that the animal creation degenerated on the American Continent. In his admirable answer to the great naturalist, Jefferson repels with spirit the allegation of the Abbé Raynal that "America has not yet produced one good poet, one skilful mathematician, one man of genius in a single art or science."[1] But he does not seem aware that the author in his edition of 1780 had already beaten a retreat from his original position.[2] This is more noteworthy as the edition appeared before the criticism.

It was after portraying the actual condition of the English Colonies in colors which aroused the protest of Jefferson that the French philosopher surrendered to a vision of the future. In reply to doubts he invokes time, education, civilization, and breaks forth : —

"Perhaps then it will be seen that America is favorable to

[1] Notes on Virginia, Query VI. Complete Works, Vol. VIII. p. 312.
[2] Liv. XVIII. chap. 32.

4

genius, to the creative arts of peace and of society. A new
Olympus, an Arcadia, an Athens, a new Greece, will produce
on the Continent, or in the archipelago which surrounds it,
Homers, Theocrituses, and especially Anacreons. Perhaps
another Newton will rise in the new Britain. It is from
English America, do not doubt, that will shoot forth the
first ray of the sciences, if they are to appear at last under a
sky so long clouded. By singular contrast with the ancient
world, where the arts passed from the South towards the
North, in the new we shall witness the North enlighten the
South. Let the English clear the land, purify the air, change
the climate, meliorate nature ; *a new universe will proceed
from their hands for the glory and happiness of humanity.*" [1]

Then, speculating on the dissensions prevailing between the Colonies and the mother country, he announces
separation, but without advantage to the European rivals
of England : —

" Break the knot which binds ancient Britain to the new ;
soon the northern colonies alone will have more power than
they possessed in union with the mother country. *This
great continent enfranchised* from all compact with Europe will
be free in all its movements. . . . . The colonies of our
absolute monarchies, following the example of the English
colonies, will themselves break the chain which binds them
shamefully to Europe." [2]

The New World opens before the prophet : —

" So everything conspires to produce the great disruption,
of which we are not permitted to foresee the precise time.
Everything tends thither, — the progress of good in the new
hemisphere and the progress of evil in the old.

[1] Tom. VI. p. 379.   Liv. XVIII. (ed. 1772).
[2] Ibid., p. 426.

"Alas! the prompt and rapid decline of our morals and our strength, the crimes of kings and the sufferings of the people, will render universal this fatal catastrophe which must detach one world from the other. The mine is preparing beneath the foundations of our rocking empires. . . . . While our people are weakening and succumbing to each other, population and agriculture are increasing in America. The arts transported by our care will quickly spring up there. This country, derived from nothing, burns to figure in turn upon the face of the globe and in the history of the world. O posterity! thou wilt be more happy, perhaps, than thy unfortunate and contemptible ancestors!"[1]

The edition of 1780 exhibits his sympathies with the Colonies. In considering the policy of the house of Bourbon, he recognizes the grasp of the pending revolution. "The United States," he says, "have shown openly the project of drawing to their confederation *all North America*"; and he mentions especially *the invitation to the people of Canada*. While questioning the conduct of France and Spain, he adds:—

"*The new hemisphere must detach itself some day from the old.* This great dismemberment is prepared in Europe by the fermentation and the shock of our opinions; by the overthrow of our rights, which created our courage; by the luxury of our courts and the wretchedness of our fields; by the hate, enduring forever, between the cowards who possess all and the robust, even the virtuous, who have nothing more to lose than life. It is prepared in America by the growth of population, of agriculture, of industry, and of intelligence. *All moves to that scission.*"[2]

In a sketch which follows are pictured the resources

[1] Tom. VI. pp. 427, 428.
[2] Liv. XVIII. chap. 52.

of the "thirteen confederate provinces" and their future development. While confessing that the name of liberty is sweet; that it is the cause of the entire human race; that revolutions in its name are a lesson to despots; that the spirit of justice, which rewards past evils by future happiness, is pleased to believe that this part of the New World cannot fail to become one of the most flourishing countries of the globe; and that some go so far as to fear *that Europe may some day find its masters in its children,*[1] he proceeds to facts which may mitigate anxiety.

The prophetic words of Raynal differ from others already quoted. Instead of letters or papers, buried in secrecy or disclosed to a few only, they were open proclamations circulated throughout Europe, and their influence began as early as 1770. A prompt translation made them known in England. In 1777 they were quoted by an English writer pleading for us.[2] Among influences coöperating with the justice of our cause, they were of constant activity, until at last France, Spain, and Holland openly united with us.

JONATHAN SHIPLEY, BISHOP OF ST. ASAPH, 1773.

Not without heartfelt emotion do I write this name, never to be mentioned by an American without a sentiment of gratitude and love. Such goodness and ability, dedicated so firmly to our cause, make Shipley conspicuous among his contemporaries. In beauty of character and in prophetic spirit he resembles Berkeley. And yet

---

[1] Liv. XVIII. chap. 52.
[2] Dr. Price, in his second tract, "Additional Observations on the Nature and Value of Civil Liberty and the War with America," p. 49, note.

biographical dictionaries forget to mention him, and in our country he is known chiefly through the friendship of Franklin. He was born about 1714, and died 9th December, 1788.

His actual preferments in the Church attest a certain success, arrested at last by his sympathy for us. At an early day John Adams spoke of him as "the best bishop that adorns the bench."[1] And we learn from Wraxall, that it was through the hostility of the king that during the short-lived Coalition Ministry Fox was prevented from making him Archbishop of Canterbury.[2] But his public life was better than any prelacy. It is impossible to read his writings without discovering the stamp of superiority, where accuracy and clearness go hand in hand with courage and truth.

The relations of Franklin with the good bishop are a beautiful episode in our revolutionary history. Two men, one English and the other American, venerable with years, mingled in friendship warm as that of youth, but steady to the grave, joining identity of sentiment on important public questions with personal affection. While Franklin remained in England, as colonial representative, watching the currents, he was a frequent guest at the Englishman's country home, and there he entered upon his incomparable autobiography, leaving behind such pleasant memories that afterwards the family never walked in the garden "without seeing Dr. Franklin's room and thinking of the work that was begun in it."[3] One of the daughters, in a

---

[1] Works, Vol. IV. p. 37. Novanglus, or a History of the Dispute with America, written in 1774.

[2] Historical Memoirs of his own Time, Vol. III. p. 347 (ed. 1836).

[3] Franklin's Works by Sparks, Vol. VIII. p. 220. Letter of Miss Catharine Louisa Shipley, 2d August, 1785.

touching letter to the latter, then at his own home in Philadelphia, informed him of her father's death, who, in reply to his "dear young friend," expressed his sense of the loss, "not to his family and friends only, but to his nation and the world," and then, after mentioning that he was in his eighty-fourth year and considerably enfeebled, added, "You will then, my dear friend, consider this as probably the last line to be received from me and as a taking leave." [1]

This brief story prepares the way for the two productions illustrating his service to us. The first has the following title: "A Sermon preached before the Incorporated Society for the Propagation of the Gospel in Foreign Parts, at their Anniversary Meeting in the Parish of St. Mary-le-Bow, on Friday, February 19, 1773." Of this discourse several editions appeared in London, New York, and Boston. [2] Lord Chatham, after confessing himself "charmed and edified" by it, wrote: "This noble discourse speaks the preacher not only fit to bear rule in the state; indeed, it does honor to the right-reverend bench." [3] Franklin, coupling it with his other productions relating to America, wrote: "Had his counsels in those pieces been attended to by the Ministers, how much bloodshed might have been prevented, and how much expense and disgrace to the nation avoided." [4]

---

[1] Franklin's Works by Sparks, Vol. X. p. 391. Letter to Miss Catharine Louisa Shipley, 27th April, 1789.

[2] One of London and another of New York are in the Congressional Library. The New York copy has the pencil lines of Mr. Webster, marking what he calls "remarkable passages" used by him in his "Address at the Laying of the Corner-stone of the Addition to the Capitol, 4th July, 1851." Works, Vol. II. p. 597.

[3] Correspondence of Earl of Chatham, Vol. IV. p. 302. Letter to Earl of Shelburne. October 24, 1773.

[4] Works by Sparks, Vol. X. p 391.

This discourse was from the text, "Glory be to God in the highest, and on earth peace, good-will towards men." [1] After announcing that "perhaps the annals of history have never afforded a more grateful spectacle to a benevolent and philosophic mind than the growth and progress of the British Colonies in North America," the preacher becomes prophet, and here his words are memorable : —

" The colonies of North America have not only taken root and acquired strength, but seem hastening with an accelerated progress to such a powerful state *as may introduce a new and important change in human affairs.*" [2]

Then picturing the Colonies as receiving " by inheritance all the improvements and discoveries of their mother country," — commencing "their flourishing state, at a time when the human understanding has attained to the free use of its powers, and has learned to act with vigor and certainty," and being in such a situation that " they may avail themselves, not only of the experience and industry, but even of the errors and mistakes, of former days," the prophet proceeds : —

" The vast continent itself, over which they are gradually spreading, may be considered a treasure yet untouched of natural productions, *that hereafter shall afford ample matter for commerce and contemplation.* And if we reflect what a stock of knowledge may be accumulated by the constant progress of industry and observation, ... *it is difficult even to imagine to what height of improvement their discoveries may extend.*" [3]

The prophet opens another vista : "And perhaps they may make as considerable *advances in the arts of*

civil government and the conduct of life." Then, exhibiting the excellences of the British Constitution with
its "equal representation," which he calls "the best discovery of political wisdom," and inquiring anxiously if
they "must rest here, as in the utmost effort of human
genius," the preacher becomes again prophetic: —

"May they not possibly be more successful than their
mother country has been in preserving that reverence and
authority which are due to the laws, — to those who make
and to those who execute them? May not a method be in-
vented of procuring some tolerable share of the comforts
of life to those inferior, useful ranks of men, to whose industry we are indebted for the whole? *Time and discipline may
discover some means to correct the extreme inequalities of condition between the rich and the poor, so dangerous to the innocence and happiness of both.*" [1]

Beautiful words! And in the same spirit the prophet
discerns increasing opportunities of progress: —

"The diversities of new scenes and situations, which so
many growing States must necessarily pass through, *may
introduce changes in the fluctuating opinions and manners of
men which we can form no conception of.* And not only the
gracious disposition of Providence, but the visible preparation of causes, *seems to indicate strong tendencies towards a
general improvement.*" [2]

To a spirit so elevated the obligations of duty are the
same for nations as for individuals, and he nobly vindicates the duty of the Christian preacher "to point out
the laws of justice and equity which must ultimately
regulate the happiness of States as well as of individuals," [3] and which he declares are no other than "those

[1] Page 8.   [2] Page 9.   [3] Page 13.

benevolent Christian morals which it is the province
of this Society to teach, transferred from the duties of
private life to the administration of public affairs."[1]
Then again he declares amazement, in which all but
hardened politicians will unite, at seeing "how slowly
in all countries the principles of natural justice, which
are so evidently necessary in private life, have been admitted into the administration of public affairs." And,
in the same spirit, he announces : —

"A time, I doubt not, will come, in the progressive improvement of human affairs, when the checks and restraints
we lay on the industry of our fellow-subjects and the jeal-
ousies we conceive at their prosperity will be considered as
the effects of a mistaken policy, prejudicial to all parties,
but chiefly to ourselves."[2]

Then, after announcing our duty "to make our country
great and powerful and rich, not by force or fraud, but
by justice, friendship, and humanity," this remarkable
sermon concludes with calling attention to "plain good
rules so often repeated to us in Scripture,"which "lie before the eyes of men, like medicinal herbs in the open
field."

In the course of his remarks, the preacher lets drop
words often quoted since and doubtless considered much
in conversation with Franklin. After setting forth that
the Colonies had been trusted, in good measure, with the
entire management of their affairs, he proceeds to say :
"And the success they have met with ought to be to us
a memorable proof that *the true art of government consists in not governing too much*."[3]

In similar spirit the good bishop came to the defence

of Massachusetts in the crisis which followed the nulli-
fication of the Tea Tax; as witness an able pamphlet,
printed in 1774, entitled "A Speech intended to have
been spoken on the Bill for altering the Charters of the
Colonies of Massachusetts Bay." In this most vigorous
production, reported by Franklin as "a masterpiece of
eloquence,"[1] where he pleads for reconciliation, after
announcing that England had drawn from the Colonies,
by commerce, "more clear profit than Spain has drawn
from all its mines,"[2] he says: "Let them continue to
enjoy the liberty our fathers gave them ! Gave them, did
I say ? They are coheirs of liberty with ourselves; and
their portion of the inheritance has been much better
looked after than ours."[3] Then again : "My Lords, I
look upon North America as the only great nursery of
freemen now left upon the face of earth."[4] And yet
once more : "But whatever may be our future fate, the
greatest glory that attends this country, a greater than
any other nation ever acquired, is to have formed and
nursed up to such a state of happiness those colonies
whom we are now so eager to butcher."[5] Thanks, perpetual thanks, to the good friend who stood so well by
our country in its beginning and discerned so clearly its
exalted future.

DEAN TUCKER, 1774.

In contrast with Shipley was his contemporary, Josiah Tucker, also of the Church, who was born 1712 and
died 4th November, 1799.

The contrast is more curious when it is considered
that Tucker, like Shipley, was for the peaceful separa-

---

[1] Letter to Mr. Coombe, July 22, 1774.   Works, Vol. VIII. p. 124.
[2] Page 15.   [3] Page 27.   [4] Page 31.   [5] Page 32.

tion of the Colonies from the mother country; but the former was biting and cynical, while the latter was sympathetic and kind. The former sent forth a succession of criticisms as from the tub of Diogenes, while the latter, with genial power, vindicated America and predicted its future. The former was a carping censor and enemy of Franklin; the latter, his loving friend.

Tucker was rector of Bristol and dean of Gloucester, and he announces that he had " written near three hundred sermons and preached them all again and again"; but it was by political essays that he made his name known and became a conspicuous gladiator.

Here it is easy to recognize industry, facility, boldness. He was not afraid to speak out, nor did he shrink from coping with those who commanded the public attention, — joining issue directly with Burke " in answer to his printed speech, *said to be spoken* in the House of Commons on the 22d of March, 1775," being that famous masterpiece, on "conciliation with America," so much read, so often quoted, and so highly placed among the efforts of human genius. The Dean used plain language, charging the great orator with excelling " in the art of ambiguous expressions," and at all times having one general end in view, " to amuse with tropes and figures and great swelling words," and hoping that while emulating the freedom of Burke in examining the writings and opinions of others, he should do it "with more decency and good manners." More than once the Dean complains that the orator had classed him by name with what he called " court vermine."

As early as 1766, in the heats of the Stamp Act, he entered the lists by an unamiable pamphlet, entitled " A Letter from a Merchant in London to his Nephew

in North America, relative to the present Posture of
Affairs in the Colonies." Here appears the vigorous
cynicism of his nature. The mother country is vindicated, and the Colonies are told that "the complaint of
being unrepresented is entirely false and groundless,"
inasmuch as every member of Parliament, when once
chosen, becomes "the equal guardian of all," and "*our*
Birminghams, Manchesters, Leeds, Halifaxes, and *your*
Bostons, New Yorks, and Philadelphias are as *really*,
though not so nominally, represented as any part whatever of the British Empire."[1] In the same spirit he
ridiculed the pretensions of colonists, putting into their
mouths the words "What! an island! A spot such as
this to command the great and mighty continent of North
America! Preposterous! A continent whose inhabitants
double every five-and-twenty years! Who, therefore,
within a century and a half, will be upwards of a hundred
and seventy millions of souls! Forbid it, patriotism, forbid it, politics, that such a great and mighty empire as
this should be held in subjection by the paltry kingdom
of Great Britain! *Rather let the seat of empire be transferred; and let it be fixed where it ought to be, namely, in
great America*";[2] and then declaring "the calculations
themselves both false and absurd,"[3] taunting the colonists with inability to make the mother country "a
province of America,"[3] and depicting the evils that
will ensue to them from separation, he announces that,
"having been surfeited with the bitter fruits of American Republicanism, they will heartily wish and petition
to be again united to the mother country."[4]

[1] A Letter from a Merchant in London to his Nephew in North America,
etc , pp. 19, 20.
[2] Ibid., p. 42.   [3] Ibid , p. 43.   [4] Ibid., p. 54.

As the conflict approached, the Dean became more earnest and incessant. In 1774 he published a book, entitled " Four Tracts on Political and Commercial Subjects," of which the third was a reprint of the " Letter from a Merchant of London," and the fourth was a new appeal, entitled " The true Interest of Great Britain set forth in regard to the Colonies, and the only Means of living in Peace and Harmony with them [including five different plans for effecting this salutary measure]." [1] Here he openly proposed separation, and predicted its advantage to England. On general grounds he was persuaded that extensive colonies were an evil rather than an advantage, especially to a commercial nation, while he was satisfied of a present alienation on the part of America, which it would be unprofitable, if not perilous, to combat. England was in no mood for such truth, and the author was set down as madman or quack. Evidently he was a prophet.

A few passages will show the character of this remarkable production.

" It is the nature of them all [colonies] to aspire after independence, and to set up for themselves as soon as ever they find that they are able to subsist without being beholden·to the mother country." [2]

True enough, and often said by others. In dealing with the different plans the Dean shows originality. To the idea of compulsion by arms he exclaimed : " But alas ! victory alone is but a poor compensation for all the blood and treasure which must be spilt." [3] The

---

[1] This Fourth Tract was published separately in Philadelphia, in 1774, with the above title.

[2] Four Tracts, p. 161.

[3] Ibid., p. 196.

plan numbered Fourth was nothing less than that
America should become the general seat of empire, and
that Great Britain and Ireland should be governed by
viceroys "from the court residences either at Philadelphia or New York or some other American imperial
city," to which the indefatigable Dean replies : —

" Now, wild as such a scheme may appear, there are certainly some Americans who seriously embrace it ; and the
late prodigious swarms of emigrants encourage them to suppose that a time is approaching when the seat of empire
must be changed.   But whatever events may be in the
womb of time, or whatever revolutions may happen in the
rise and fall of empires, there is not the least probability
that this country should ever become a province to North
America. . . . . Unless, indeed, we should add one extravagance to another, by supposing that the Americans are to
conquer all the world, and in that case I do allow that England must become a province to America. " [1]

Then comes the Fifth Plan, which was "to separate
entirely from the North American Colonies by declaring
them to be a free and independent people, over whom
we lay no claim, and then by offering to guarantee this
freedom and independence against all foreign invaders
whatever." [2]   And he proceeds to show that by such
separation the mother country would not lose the trade
of the Colonies.   His unamiable nature flares out in the
suggestion that "the moment a separation takes effect,
intestine quarrels will begin " ; [3] that " in proportion as
their republican spirit shall intrigue and cabal, they will
split into parties, divide and subdivide," while his confidence in the result is declared ; "and yet I have ob-

---

[1] Four Tracts, p. 201.   [2] Ibid., p. 203.   [3] Ibid., p. 219.

served, and have myself had some experience, that measures evidently right will prevail at last"; therefore he had not the least doubt but that a separation would take place "within half a century."[1] Though seeing the separation so clearly, he did not see how near at hand it then was.

The Dean grew more earnest. Other pamphlets followed; for instance, in 1775, "An Humble Address and Earnest Appeal, whether a Connection with or a Separation from the Continental Colonies of America be most for the National Advantage and the lasting Benefit of these Kingdoms." Here he says openly: —

"My scheme, which Mr. Burke is pleased to term a childish one, is to separate totally from the Colonies, and to reject them from being fellow-members and joint-partakers with us in the privileges and advantages of the British Empire, because they refuse to submit to the authority and jurisdiction of the British legislature, — offering at the same time to enter into alliances of friendship and treaties of commerce with them, as with any other sovereign, independent state."[2]

Then, insisting that his scheme "most infallibly cuts off all the present causes of dispute and contention between the two countries, so that they never can revive again,"[3] he establishes that commercial intercourse with the Americans would not cease, inasmuch as it cannot be shown that they "will no longer adhere to their own interest when they shall be disunited from us."[4]

Among subsequent tracts was one entitled "Cui Bono? Or an Inquiry what Benefits can arrive either to

[1] Four Tracts, p. 221.
[2] Page 5.   [3] Page 29.   [4] Page 48.

England or the Americans, the French, Spaniards, or
Dutch, from the greatest Victories or Successes in the
present War, being a Series of Letters addressed to
Monsieur Necker, late Controller-General of the Finances
of France. Printed at Glocester, 1782." Here was the
same ardor for separation, with the same bitter words
for the Colonies.

Tardily the foresight of the Dean was recognized,
until at last Archbishop Whately, in his annotation
upon Bacon's Essay on Honor and Reputation commemorates it as an historic example. According to him
" the whole British nation were in one particular mani-
festly *puzzle-headed*, except *one* man, who was accord-
ingly derided by all." Then mentioning the dispute
between the mother country and her colonies, he says:
" But Dean Tucker, standing quite alone, wrote a pamphlet to show that the separation would be no loss at
all, and that we had best give them the independence
they coveted at once and in a friendly way. Some
thought he was writing in jest; the rest despised him
as too absurd to be worth answering. But now, and
for above half a century, every one admits that he was
quite right, and regrets that his view was not adopted." [1]
Unquestionably this is a remarkable tribute. Kindred
to it was that of the excellent Professor Smyth, who, in
exhibiting the " American War," dwells on " the superior and the memorable wisdom of Tucker." [2]

The bad temper shooting from his writings interfered,
doubtless, with their acceptance. His spirit, so hostile
to us, justified his own characterization of himself as
" the author of these tracts against the rebel Ameri-

[1] Bacon's Essays, by Whately, p. 486.
[2] Lectures on Modern History. Vol. II. p. 380, Lecture XXXII.

cans." As the war drew to a close, his bad temper still prevailed, heightened by antipathy to republicanism, so that, after picturing the Colonies, separated at last from the mother country, as having " gained a general disappointment mixed with anger and indignation,"[1] he thus predicts their terrible destiny : —

" As to the future grandeur of America and its being a rising empire under one Head, whether republican or monarchical, it is one of the idlest and most visionary notions that ever was conceived, even by writers of romance. For there is nothing in the genius of the people, the situation of their country, or the nature of their different climates, which tends to countenance such a supposition. . . . . Above all, when those immense inland regions beyond the back settlements, which are still unexplored, are taken into the account, they form the highest probability that the Americans never can be united into one compact empire, under any species of government whatever. Their fate seems to be — *a disunited people till the end of time.*"[2]

Alas! But evidently the Dean saw the future of our continent no better than the Ministry saw their duty with regard to it.

Unlike in spirit was Mathew Robinson, a contemporary friend of America, whose able and elaborate tracts[3] in successive editions are now forgotten except so far as revived by the praise of Professor Smyth.[4] His vindi-

1 Cui Bono ? p. 86.

2 Ibid , pp. 117, 118.

3 Considerations on the Measures carrying on with respect to the British Colonies in North America, 1774. A further Examination of our present American Measures and of the Reasons and Principles on which they are founded, 1776.

4 Lectures on Modern History, Vol. II. p. 383, Lecture XXXII.

cation of the Colonies, at the time of the Boston Port
Bill, was complete, without the harshness of Tucker,
and he did not hesitate to present the impossibility of
conquering them. "What expectation or probability,"
he asks, "can there be of sending from hence armies
capable to conquer and subdue so great a force of men
defending and defended by such a continent."[1] Then,
while depicting English mastery of the sea, he says:
"We may do whatever a fleet can. Very true; but it
cannot sail all over North America."[2] The productions of
this enlightened author cannot have been without effect.
Doubtless they helped the final acknowledgment of
independence. When will the "Old Mortality" appear
to discover and restore his monument?

The able annotator of Lord Bacon was too sweeping
when he said that on the great American question all
England was wrong "except *one* man."[3] Robinson was
as right as the Dean, and there were others also. The
"Monthly Review," in an article on the Dean's appeal
for separation, said: "This, however, is not a new idea.
It has frequently occurred to others."[4] Even Soames
Jenyns, a life-long member of Parliament, essayist, poet,
defender of Christianity, while upholding the right to
tax the Colonies, is said to have accepted the idea of
"total separation."

> "Let all who view th' instructive scene,
>   And patronize the plan,
> Give thanks to Gloucester's honest Dean,
>   For, Tucker, thou 'rt the man."[5]

[1] Considerations, p. 66.
[2] Ibid., p. 72.
[3] Bacon's Essays, by Whately, p. 486.
[4] February, 1774, Vol. I. p. 135.
[5] The American Coachman, Jenyns's Works, Vol. I. p. 205. The editor,
not regarding this little poem as a jest, says of it : "The author, with that

In a better spirit and with affecting earnestness, John Cartwright, once of the Royal Navy and known as Major from his rank in the Nottinghamshire Militia, followed the Dean, in 1774, with a series of letters collected in a pamphlet entitled "American Independence, the Interest and Glory of Great Britain," where he insists upon separation, and thenceforward a friendly league, "that the true and lasting welfare of both countries can be promoted." In enforcing his conclusion the author says: "When we talk of asserting our sovereignty over the Americans, do we foresee to what fatal lengths it will carry us? Are not those nations increasing with astonishing rapidity? *Must they not, in the nature of things, cover in a few ages that immense continent like a swarm of bees?*"[1] Then again: "We may, indeed, by means of fleets and armies, maintain a precarious tyranny over the Americans for a while; but the most shallow politicians must foresee what this would end in."[2] Then in reply to the Dean: "'T is a pity so able a writer had not discovered that the Americans have a right to choose their own governors, and thence enforce the necessity of his proposed separation as a religious duty, no less than a measure of national policy."[3] Cartwright continued at home the conflicts of principle involved in our war of independence, and became an English Reformer. Honor to his name!

conciseness as to the matter and humor in the manner so peculiar to himself, recommends and supports the Dean's plan."

[1] Page 65, Letter VI., March 27, 1774.
[2] Ibid., p. 66.
[3] Ibid., p. 68.

DAVID HARTLEY, 1775, 1785.

ANOTHER English friend was David Hartley. He was constant and even pertinacious on our side, although less prophetic than Pownall, with whom he coöperated in purpose and activity. His father was Hartley the metaphysician, and author of the ingenious theory of sensation, who predicted the fate of existing governments and hierarchies in two simple sentences: " It is probable that all the civil governments will be overturned "; " it is probable that the present forms of church government will be dissolved." Many were alarmed. Lady Charlotte Wentworth asked the prophet when these terrible things would happen. The answer was: " I am an old man, and shall not live to see them ; but you are a young woman, and will probably see them." [1]

The son was born in 1729, and died at Bath in 1813. During our Revolution he sat in Parliament for Kingston-upon-Hull. He was also the British plenipotentiary in negotiating the definitive Treaty of Peace with the United States. He has dropped out of sight. The biographical dictionaries afford him a few lines only. But he deserves a considerable place in the history of our independence.

John Adams was often austere, and sometimes cynical in his judgments. Evidently he did not like Hartley. In one place he speaks of him as " talkative and disputatious, and not always intelligible " ; [2] then, as " a person of consummate vanity " ; [3] and then, when

---

[1] D'Israeli's Curiosities of Literature, Vol. III. p. 275. Predictions.
[2] Works, Vol. IX. p. 517.
[3] Ibid., Vol. III. p. 137.

appointed to sign the definitive Treaty, "it would have been more agreeable to have finished with Mr. Oswald";[1] and, in still another place, "Mr. Hartley was as copious as usual."[2] And yet, when writing most elaborately to Count de Vergennes on the prospects of the negotiation with England, he introduces opinions of Hartley at length, saying that he was "more for peace than any man in the kingdom."[3] Such testimony may well outweigh the other expressions, especially as nothing of the kind appears in the correspondence of Franklin, with whom Hartley was much more intimate.

The Parliamentary History is a sufficient monument for Hartley. He was a frequent speaker, and never missed an opportunity of pleading our cause. Although without the immortal eloquence of Burke, he was always clear and full. Many of his speeches seem written out by himself. He was not a tardy convert, but began as "a new member" by supporting an amendment favorable to the Colonies, 5th December, 1774. Then, in March, 1775, he brought forward "propositions for conciliation with America," which he sustained in an elaborate speech, where he avowed that the American Question had occupied him for some time: —

"Though I have so lately had the honor of a seat in this House, yet I have for many years turned my thoughts and attention to matters of public concern and national policy. This question of America is now of many years' standing."[4]

In this speech he acknowledges the services of New England at Louisburg: —

[1] Works, Vol. VII. p. 54.
[2] Ibid., Vol. III. p. 363.
[3] Ibid., Vol. VII. p 226.
[4] Parliamentary History. Vol. XVIII. p. 553.

"In that war too, sir, they took Louisburg from the French, single-handed, without any European assistance, — as mettled an enterprise as any in our history, — an everlasting memorial of the zeal, courage, and perseverance of the troops of New England. The men themselves dragged the cannon over a morass which had always been thought impassable, where neither horses nor oxen could go, and they carried the shot upon their backs. And what was their reward for this forward and spirited enterprise, — for the reduction of this American Dunkirk? Their reward, sir, you know very well; it was given up for a barrier to the Dutch." [1]

All his various propositions were negatived; but he was not disheartened. Constantly he spoke, — now on the budget, then on the address, and then on specific propositions. At this time he asserted the power of Parliament over the Colonies, and he proposed, on the 2d November, 1775, that a test of submission by the Colonists should be the recognition of an act of Parliament " enacting that all the slaves in America should have the trial by jury." [2] Shortly afterwards, on the 5th December, 1775, he brought forward a second set of " propositions for conciliation with America," where, among other things, he embodied the test on slavery, which he put forward as a compromise; and here his language belongs, not only to the history of our Revolution, but to the history of antislavery. While declaring that in his opinion Great Britain was " the aggressor in everything," he sought to bring the two countries together on a platform of human rights, which he thus explained : —

" The act to be proposed to America, *as an auspicious beginning to lay the first stone of universal liberty to mankind,*

1 Parliamentary History, Vol. XVIII. p. 556.
2 Ibid., p. 846.

should be what no American could hesitate an instant to comply with, namely, that every slave in North America should be entitled to his trial by jury in all criminal cases. America cannot refuse to accept and enroll such an act as this, and thereby to reëstablish peace and harmony with the parent State. *Let us all be reunited in this, as a foundation to extirpate slavery from the face of the earth. Let those who seek justice and liberty for themselves give that justice and liberty to their fellow-creatures.* With respect to putting a final period to slavery in North America, it should seem best that, when this country had led the way by the act for jury, each Colony, knowing their own peculiar circumstances, should undertake the work in the most practicable way, and that they should endeavor to establish some system by which slavery should be in a certain term of years abolished. *Let the only contention henceforward between Great Britain and America be, which shall exceed the other in zeal for establishing the fundamental rights of liberty for all mankind."* [1]

How grand and beautiful, not to be read without gratitude! The motion was rejected; but among the twenty-three in its favor were Fox and Burke. During this same month the unwearied defender of our country came forward again, declaring that he could not be "an adviser or a well-wisher to any of the vindictive operations against America, because the cause is unjust; but at the same time he must be equally earnest to secure British interests from destruction," and he thus prophesies : —

"The fate of America is cast. You may bruise its heel, but you cannot crush its head. It will revive again. *The new world is before them. Liberty is theirs.* They have pos-

[1] Parliamentary History, Vol. XVIII. p. 1050.

session of a free government, their birthright and inheritance, derived to them from their parent state, which the
hand of violence cannot wrest from them. If you will cast
them off, my last wish is to them, May they go and pros-
per !"

Again, on the 10th May, 1776, he vindicated anew
his original proposition, and here again he testifies for
peace and against slavery.

" For the sake of peace, therefore, I did propose a test of
compromise by an act of acceptance, on the part of the
Colonists, of an act of Parliament which should lay *the
foundation for the extirpation of the horrid custom of slavery
in the New World.* My motion was simply an act of compromise and reconciliation ; and, as far as it was a legisla-
tive act, it was still to have been applied in correcting the
laws of slavery in America, which I considered as repugnant
to the laws of the realm of England and to the fundamen-
tals of our constitution. Such a compromise would at the
same time have saved the national honor." [1]

All gratitude to the hero who at this early day
vowed himself to the abolition of slavery. Hartley is
among the first of abolitionists, with hardly a predecessor except Granville Sharp, and in Parliament absolute-
ly the first. Clarkson was at this time fifteen years old,
Wilberforce sixteen. Only in 1787 Clarkson obtained
the prize for the best Latin essay on the question, " Is
it right to make men slaves against their will ?" It
was not until 1791 that Wilberforce moved for leave to
bring in a bill for the abolition of the slave-trade. It
is no small honor for one man to have come forward in

---

[1] Parliamentary History, Vol. XVIII. p. 1356.

Parliament as an avowed abolitionist, while at the same time a vindicator of our independence.

Again, on the 15th May, 1777, Hartley pleaded for us : —

"At sea, which has hitherto been our prerogative element, they rise against us at a stupendous rate; and if we cannot return to our old mutual hospitalities towards each other, a very few years will show us a most formidable hostile marine, ready to join hands with any of our enemies. . . . . I will venture to prophesy that the principles of a federal alliance are the only terms of peace that ever will and that ever ought to obtain between the two countries."[1]

On the 15th of June, immediately afterwards, the Parliamentary History reports briefly : —

"Mr. Hartley went upon the cruelties of slavery, and urged the Board of Trade to take some means of mitigating it. He produced a pair of handcuffs, which he said was a manufacture they were now going to establish."[2]

Thus again the abolitionist reappeared in the vindicator of our independence. On the 22d June, 1779, he brought forward another formal motion " for reconciliation with America," and, in the course of a well-considered speech, denounced the ministers for "headstrong and inflexible obstinacy in prosecuting a cruel and destructive American war."[3] On the 3d December, 1779, in what is called "a very long speech," he returned to his theme, inveighing against ministers for " the favorite, though wild, Quixotic, and impracticable

[1] Parliamentary History, Vol. XIX. pp. 259, 260.
[2] Ibid., p. 315.
[3] Ibid., p. 904.

5   G

measure of coercing America." [1]   These are only instances.

During this time he maintained relations with Franklin, as appears in the "Diplomatic Correspondence of the Revolution," all of which attests a desire for peace.   In 1778 he arrived at Paris on a confidential errand, especially to confer with Franklin.   On this occasion John Adams met him and judged him severely.   In 1783 he was appointed a commissioner to sign the definitive Treaty of Peace.

These things belong to history.   Though perhaps not generally known, they are accessible.   I have presented them for their intrinsic value and prophetic character, but also as the introduction to an unpublished letter from Hartley, which I received some time ago from an English friend who has since been called away from important labors.   The letter concerns *emigration to our country and the payment of the national debt.*

The following indorsement explains its character: —

"*Note.*   This is a copy of the material portion of a long letter from D. Hartley, the British Commissioner in Paris, to Lord Sydenham, January, 1785.   The original was sold by C. Robinson, of 21 Bond Street, London, on the 6th April, 1859, at a sale of Hartley's MSS. and papers chiefly relating to the United States of America.   It was Hartley's copy, in his own hand.

"The lot was No. 82 in the sale catalogue.   It was bought by J. R. Smith, the London bookseller, for £2 6s. 0d.

"I had a copy made before the sale.

                                        "*Joseph Parkes.*
"LONDON, 18 July, '59."

[1] Parliamentary History, Vol. XIX. p. 1190.

The letter is as follows : —

"My Lord, — In your Lordship's last letter to me, just before my leaving Paris, you are pleased to say that any information which I might have been able to collect of a nature to promote the mutual and reciprocal interests of Great Britain and the United States of America would be extremely acceptable to his Majesty's government. . . . . Annexed to this letter I have the honor of transmitting to your Lordship some papers and documents which I have received from the American Ministers. One of them (No. 5) is a Map of the Continent of North America, in which the land ceded to them by the late treaty of peace is divided, by parallels of latitude and longitude, into fourteen new States.

"The whole project, in its full extent, would take many years in its execution, and therefore it must be far beyond the present race of men to say, 'This shall be so.' Nevertheless, *those who have the first care of this New World will probably give it such directions and inherent influences as may guide and control its course and revolutions for ages to come.* But these plans, being beyond the reach of man to predestinate, are likewise beyond the reach of comment or speculation to say what may or may not be possible, or to predict what events may hereafter be produced by time, climates, soils, adjoining nations, or by the unwieldy magnitude of empire, and *the future population of millions superadded to millions.* The sources of the Mississippi may be unknown. The lines of longitude and latitude may be extended into unexplored regions, and the plan of this new creation may be sketched out by a presumptuous compass, if all its intermediate uses and functions were to be suspended until the final and precise accomplishment, without failure or deviation, of this unbounded plan. But this is not the case ; the immediate objects in view are limited and precise ; they are

of prudent thought, and within the scope of human power
to measure out and to execute. The principle indeed is in-
definite, and will be left to the test of future ages to determine its duration or extent.

" I take the liberty to suggest thus much, lest we should
be led away to suppose that the councils which have produced these plans have had no wiser or more sedate views
than merely the amusement of drawing meridians of ambition and high thoughts. There appear to me to be two
solid and rational objects in view : the first is, by the sale
of lands nearly contiguous to the present States (receiving
Congress paper in payment according to its scale of depreci-
ation) *to extinguish the present national debt,* which I understand might be discharged for about twelve millions sterling. . . . .

" It is a new proposition to be offered to the numerous
common rank of mankind in all the countries of the world,
to say that there are in America fertile soils and temperate
climates in which an acre of land may be purchased for a
trifling consideration, which may be possessed in freedom,
together with all the natural and civil rights of mankind.
The Congress have already proclaimed this, and that no
other qualification or name is necessary but to become
settlers, without distinction of countries or persons. The
European peasant, who toils for his scanty sustenance in
penury, wretchedness, and servitude, will eagerly fly to this
asylum for free and industrious labor. The tide of immigration may set strongly outward from Scotland, Ireland,
and Canada to this new land of promise.

" A very great proportion of men in all the countries of
the world are without property, and generally are subject
to governments of which they have no participation, and
over whom they have no control. The Congress have now
opened to all the world a sale of landed settlements where
the liberty and property of each individual is to be con-

signed to his own custody and defence. . . . . These are such propositions of free establishments as have never yet been offered to mankind, and cannot fail of producing great effects in the future progress of things. The Congress have arranged their offers in the most inviting and artful terms, and lest individual peasants and laborers should not have the means of removing themselves, they throw out inducements to moneyed adventurers to purchase and to undertake the settlement by commission and agency, without personal residence, by stipulating that the lands of proprietors being absentees shall not be higher taxed than the lands of residents. This will quicken the sale of lands, which is their object.

" For the explanation of these points, I beg leave to refer your Lordship to the documents annexed, Nos. 5 and 6, namely, the Map and Resolutions of Congress, dated April, 1784. Another circumstance would confirm that it is the intention of Congress to invite moneyed adventurers to make purchases and settlements, which is the precise and mathematical mode of dividing and marking out for sale the lands in each new proposed State. These new States are to be divided by parallel lines running north and south, and by other parallels running east and west. They are to be divided into hundreds of ten geographical miles square, and then again into lots of one square mile. The divisions are laid out as regularly as the squares upon a chessboard, and all to be formed into a Charter of Compact.

" They may be purchased by purchasers at any distance, and the titles may be verified by registers of such or such numbers, north or south, east or west ; all this is explained by the document annexed, No. 7, viz. *The Ordinance for ascertaining the mode of locating and disposing of lands in the Western Territory. This is their plan and means for paying off their national debt, and they seem very intent upon doing it.* I should observe that their debt consists of two parts, namely, domestic and foreign. The sale of lands is to be appropriated to the former.

"The domestic debt may perhaps be nine or ten millions, and the foreign debt two or three. For payment of the foreign debt it is proposed to lay a tax of five per cent upon all imports until discharged, which, I am informed, has already been agreed to by most of the States, and probably will soon be confirmed by the rest. Upon the whole, it appears that this plan is as prudently conceived and as judiciously arranged, as to the end proposed, as any experienced cabinet of European ministers could have devised or planned any similar project.

"The second point which appears to me to be deserving of attention, respecting the immense cession of territory to the United States at the late peace, is a point *which will perhaps in a few years become an unparalleled phenomenon in the political world.* As soon as the national debt of the United States shall be discharged by the sale of one portion of those lands, we shall then see the Confederate Republic in a new character, as a proprietor of lands, either for sale or to let upon rents, while other nations may be struggling under debts too enormous to be discharged either by economy or taxation, and while they may be laboring to raise ordinary and necessary supplies by burdensome impositions upon their own persons and properties. *Here will be a nation possessed of a new and unheard-of financial organ of stupendous magnitude, and in process of time of unmeasured value, thrown into their lap as a fortuitous superfluity, and almost without being sought for.*

. "When such an organ of revenue begins to arise into produce and exertion, what public uses it may be applicable to, or to what abuses and perversions it might be rendered subservient, is far beyond the reach of probable discussion now. Such discussions would only be visionary speculations. However, thus far it is obvious and highly deserving of our attention that it cannot fail becoming to the American States a most important instrument of national power, the progress and operation of which must hereafter be *a most interesting object of attention to the British American dominions which are in close vicinity to the territories of the United States, and I should hope that these considerations would lead us, inasmuch as we value those parts of our dominions, to encourage conciliatory and amicable correspondence between them and their neighbors.*"

This private communication, now for the first time seeing the light, is full of prophecy, or of that remarkable discernment and forecast which mark the prophetic spirit, whether in announcing "the future population of millions superadded to millions," or in the high estimate of the National Territory, destined to become in a few years "an unparalleled phenomenon in the political world," — "a new and unheard-of *financial organ* of stupendous magnitude." How few at home saw the Public Lands with as clear a vision as Hartley!

GALIANI, 1776, 1778.

AMONG the most brilliant in this extending list is the Abbé Galiani, the Neapolitan, who was born 1728, and died at Naples 1787. Although Italian by birth, yet by the accident of official residence he became for a while domesticated in France, wrote the French language, and now enjoys a French reputation. His writings in French and his letters have the wit and ease of Voltaire.

Galiani was a genius. Whatever he touched shone at once with his brightness, in which there was originality as well as knowledge. He was a finished scholar,

and very successful in lapidary verses. Early in life,
while in Italy, he wrote a grave essay on Money, which
contrasted with another of rare humor suggested by
the death of the public executioner. Other essays
followed, and then came the favor of the congenial
pontiff, Benedict XIV. In 1760 he found himself at
Paris as Secretary of the Neapolitan Embassy. Mingling with courtiers officially, according to the duties
of his position, he fraternized with the liberal and
adventurous spirits who exercised such influence over
society and literature. He was recognized as one of
them, and inferior to none. His petty stature was forgotten, when he conversed with inexhaustible faculties
of all kinds, so that he seemed an Encyclopædia, Harle-
quin, and Machiavelli all in one. The atheists at the
Thursday dinner of D'Holbach were confounded, while
he enforced the existence of God. Into the questions
of political economy occupying attention at the time
he entered with a pen which seemed borrowed from
the French Academy. His *Dialogues sur le Commerce
des Blés* had the success of a romance; ladies carried
this book on corn in their work-baskets. Returning to
Naples, he continued to live in Paris through his correspondence, especially with Madame d'Épinay, the Baron
d'Holbach, Diderot, and Grimm.[1]

Among later works, after his return to Naples, was
a solid volume — not to be forgotten in the History
of International Law — on the "Rights of Neutrals,"
where a difficult subject is treated with such mastery
that, half a century later, D'Hautefeuille, in his elaborate treatise, copies from it at length. Galiani was the

---

[1] Biographie Universelle of Michaud; also of Didot; Louis Blanc, Histoire de la Révolution Française, Tom. I. pp. 390, 545 – 551.

predecessor of this French writer in the extreme assertion of neutral rights. Other works were left at his
death in manuscript, some grave and some humorous;
also letters without number. The letters preserved
from Italian *savans* filled eight large volumes; those
from *savans*, ministers, and sovereigns abroad filled fourteen. His Parisian correspondence did not see the light
till 1818, although some of the letters may be found
in the contemporary correspondence of Grimm.

In his Parisian letters, which are addressed chiefly
to that clever individuality, Madame d'Épinay, the
Neapolitan abbé shows not only the brilliancy and
nimbleness of his talent, but the universality of his
knowledge and the boldness of his speculations. Here
are a few words from a letter dated at Naples, 12th
October, 1776, in which he brings forward the idea of
"races," so important in our day, with an illustration
from Russia: —

"*All depends on races.* The first, the most noble of
races, comes naturally from the North of Asia. The Rus-
sians are the nearest to it, and this is the reason why
they have made more progress in fifty years than can be
got out of the Portuguese in five hundred." [1]

Belonging to the Latin race, Galiani was entitled to
speak thus freely.

In another letter to Madame d'Épinay, dated at
Naples, 18th May, 1776, he had already foretold the
success of our Revolution. Few prophets have been
more explicit than he was in the following passage: —

"Livy said of his age, which so much resembled ours,
'Ad hæc tempora ventum est quibus, nec vitia nostra, nec

---

[1] Correspondance, Tom. II. p. 221. See also Grimm, Correspondance,
Tom. IX. p. 282.

5 *

remedia pati possumus,' — 'We are in an age where the remedies hurt as much as the vices.' Do you know the reality? *The epoch has come of the total fall of Europe, and of transmigration into America.* All here turns into rottenness, — religion, laws, arts, sciences, — and all hastens to renew itself in America. This is not a jest; nor is it an idea drawn from the English quarrels; I have said it, announced it, preached it, for more than twenty years, and I have constantly seen my prophecies come to pass. *Therefore, do not buy your house in the Chaussée d'Antin; you must buy it in Philadelphia.* My trouble is that there are no abbeys in America."[1]

This letter was written some months before the Declaration of Independence was known in Europe.

In another, dated at Naples, 7th February, 1778, the Abbé alludes to the "quantities" of English men and women who have come to Naples "for shelter from the American tempest," and adds, "Meanwhile the Washingtons and Hancocks will be fatal to them."[2] In still another, dated at Naples, 25th July, 1778, he renews his prophecies in language still more explicit : —

"You will at this time have decided the greatest revolution of the globe; namely, *if it is America which is to reign over Europe, or if it is Europe which is to continue to reign over America.* I will wager in favor of America, for the reason merely physical, that for five thousand years genius has turned opposite to the diurnal motion, and travelled from the East to the West."[3]

Here again is the idea of Berkeley which has been so captivating.

---

[1] Correspondance, Tom. II. p. 203; Grimm, Tom. IX. p. 285.
[2] Correspondance, Tom. II. p. 275.
[3] Ibid., Tom. II. p. 275.

ADAM SMITH, 1776.

In contrast with the witty Italian is the illustrious philosopher and writer of Scotland, Adam Smith, who was born 5th June, 1723, and died 17th July, 1790. His fame is so commanding that any details of life or works would be out of place. He was thinker and inventor, through whom mankind was advanced in knowledge.

I say nothing of his "Theory of Moral Sentiments," constituting an important contribution to the science of ethics, but come at once to his great work of political economy, entitled "Inquiry into the Nature and Sources of the Wealth of Nations," which first appeared in 1776. Its publication marks an epoch described by Mr. Buckle when he says :[1] "Adam Smith contributed more, by the publication of this single work, toward the happiness of man, than has been effected by the united abilities of all the statesmen and legislators of whom history has preserved an authentic account." The work is full of prophetic knowledge, and especially with regard to the British colonies. Writing while the debate with the mother country was still pending, Adam Smith urged that they should be admitted to Parliamentary representation in proportion to taxation, so that their representation would enlarge with their growing resources; and here he predicts nothing less than the transfer of empire.

"The distance of America from the seat of government, the natives of that country might flatter themselves, with some appearance of reason too, would not be of very long

[1] History of Civilization in England, Vol. I. p. 216.

continuance. Such has hitherto been the rapid progress of that country in wealth, population, and improvement, that, in the course of little more than a century, perhaps, the produce of America might exceed that of British taxation. *The seat of the empire would then naturally remove itself to that part of the empire which contributed most to the general defence and support of the whole."* [1]

In these tranquil words of assured science the great author carries the seat of government across the Atlantic.

Did Adam Smith in this remarkable passage do more than follow a hint from our own prophet? The prophecy of the great economist first appeared in 1776. In the course of 1774 and down to April 19, 1775, John Adams published in the Boston Gazette a series of weekly articles under the signature of Novanglus, which were abridged in Almon's Remembrancer for 1775, with the following title, "History of the Dispute with America, from its origin in 1754 to the present time." Although this abridged edition stops before the prophetic passage, it is not impossible that the whole series was known to Adam Smith. After speculating, as the latter did afterwards, on the extension of the British Constitution and Parliamentary representation to the outlying British dominions, our prophet says : —

"If in twenty years more America should have six millions of inhabitants, as there is a boundless territory to fill up, she must have five hundred representatives. Upon these principles, if in forty years she should have twelve millions, a thousand ; and if the inhabitants of the three kingdoms remain as they are, being already full of inhabi-

[1] Wealth of Nations, Book IV. cap. 7, part 3.

tants, what will become of your supreme legislature? *It will be translated, crown and all, to America.* This is a sublime system for America. It will flatter those ideas of independency which the Tories impute to them, if they have any such, more than any other plan of independency that I have ever heard projected."[1]

Thus plainly was John Adams precursor of Adam Smith.

These papers were reprinted without abridgment in London, in 1784, by Stockdale, with the title "History of the Disputes with America from their origin in 1754, written in the year 1774." The Monthly Review, in a notice of the publication, after speaking of "the inauspicious system of American taxation," says, "Mr. Adams foretold the consequence of obstinately adhering to it, and the event hath too well verified his predictions. They were, however, predictions which required no inspiration."[2] So that his wise second sight was recognized in England much beyond the prevision of Adam Smith.

The idea of transporting the seat of government to America was often attributed to Franklin by Dean Tucker. The former in a letter, as early as 25th November, 1767, reports the Dean as saying, "That is his constant plan."[3] In one of his tracts,[4] the Dean attributes it not only to Franklin, but also to our people. With strange exaggeration he says: "It has been the unanimous opinion of the North Americans for these fifty years past, that the seat of empire ought to be

---

[1] Works, Vol. IV. pp. 4, 101, 102; Almon's Remembrancer.

[2] 1784, Vol. I. p. 478.

[3] Works by Sparks, Vol. VII. p. 366.

[4] Answers to certain Popular Objections against separating from the Rebellious Colonies. Glocester, 1776.

transferred from the lesser to the greater country, that
is, from England to America, or as Dr. Franklin elegantly phrased it, from the cock-boat to the man-of-war." [1]
It is impossible to say how much of this was from the
excited brain of the Dean.[2]

DR. RICHARD PRICE, 1776, 1777, 1778, 1784.

A TRUE and solid ally of our country at a critical period was Dr. Price, dissenting clergyman, metaphysician,
political writer, and mathematician, who was born in
Wales, 23d February, 1723, and died in London, 17th
March, 1791.

His earliest labors were a " Review of the Principal
Questions and Difficulties in Morals," by which he was
recognized as a metaphysician, and a " Treatise on Re-
versionary Payments," by which he was recognized as
an authority on a large class of financial questions. At
the same time his sermons were regarded as excellent.
Amidst these various labors he was moved to enlist as a
pamphleteer in defence of the American Colonies. This
service, prompted by a generous devotion to just principles, awakened grateful sentiments on both sides of the
ocean.

The Common Council of London marked its sympathy by voting him the freedom of the city in a gold box
of £50 value. The American Congress sent him a different testimonial, officially communicated to him, being
a solemn resolution declaring " the desire of Congress to
consider him as a citizen of the United States, and to
receive his assistance in regulating their finances." [3] In

---

[1] Page 59.
[2] See also Cui Bono? p. 87.
[3] John Adams, Works, Vol. VII. p. 71.

reply, under date of 18th January, 1779, while declining
the invitation, he offered "assurances that Dr. Price
feels the warmest gratitude for the notice taken of him,
and that he looks to the American States as *now* the
hope and likely *soon* to become the refuge of mankind." [1]
Franklin and Adams contracted with him relations of
friendship. The former, under date of 6th February, 1780,
wrote him: "Your writings, after all the abuse you
and they have met with, begin to make serious impressions on those who at first rejected the counsels you
gave." [2]   And 2d October, 1788, he wrote to another:
" Remember me affectionately to good Dr. Price." [3] The
latter, in correspondence many years afterwards, recorded
the intimacy he enjoyed with Dr. Price at the house of
the latter, " at his own house and at the houses and
tables of many friends." [4]

The first of his American tracts was in 1776, being
" Observations on the Nature of Civil Liberty, the Principles of Government, and the Justice and Policy of the
War with America." The sale of sixty thousand copies
in a few months shows the extensive acceptance of the
work. The general principles so clearly exhibited are
invoked for America. Occasionally the philosopher becomes prophet, as when he predicts the growth of population : —

" They are now but little short of half our number. To
this number they have grown from a small body of original
settlers by a very rapid increase. The probability is that
they will go on to increase, and that in fifty or sixty years
they will be *double our number and form a mighty empire*,

1 Writings of Franklin by Sparks, Vol. VIII. p. 355.
2 Ibid., p. 417.
3 Ibid., Vol. X. p. 365.
4 Letter to Jefferson, September 14, 1813. Works, Vol. X. p. 175.

consisting of a variety of States, all equal or superior to our-
selves in all the arts and accomplishments which give dignity
and happiness to human life." [1]

Nothing less than "a vast continent" seems to him the
sphere of this remarkable development, and he revolts
at the idea of this being held "at the discretion of a
handful of people on the other side of the Atlantic."
In the measures which brought on the war he saw "the
hand of Providence *working to bring about some great
end.*" [2]   And the vast continent was to be dedicated to
Liberty.   The excellent man saw even the end of slavery.   Speaking of "the negroes of the southern colonies,"
he said that they "probably will have either soon become
extinct or *have their condition changed into that of freemen.*" [3]   Years and battle intervened before this precious
result.

This production was followed in 1777 by "Additional Observations on the Nature and Value of Civil
Liberty and the War with America," to which were
added "Observations on Public Loans, the National
Debt, and the Debt and Resources of France."   In all
this variety of topics, his concern for America breaks
forth in the inquiry, "Must not humanity shudder at
such a war?"   And he sees untold loss to England,
which, with the Colonies, "might be the greatest and
happiest nation that ever existed"; but without them
"we are no more one people; our existence depends on
keeping them."   This patriotic gloom is checked by another vision : —

"These measures have, in all probability, hastened the
disruption of the new from the old world, *which will begin a*

---

[1] Pages 25, 26.   [2] Page 55.   [3] Page 41, note.

new era in the annals of mankind, and produce a revolution more important, perhaps, than any that has happened in human affairs." [1]

Thus was American independence heralded and its influence foretold.

Constantly sympathizing with America, and impressed by the magnitude of the issue, his soul found another utterance in 1778, in what he called "The General Introduction to the Two Tracts on Civil Liberty, the War with America, and the Finances of the Kingdom." Here again he sees a vision : —

"A great people, likely to be formed, in spite of all our efforts, into free communities, under governments which have no religious tests and establishments! A new era in future annals, and a new opening in human affairs, beginning among the descendants of Englishmen, in a new world! *A rising empire, extended over an immense continent, without bishops, without nobles, and without kings.*" [2]

After the recognition of Independence and the establishment of peace, Dr. Price appeared with another tract: "Observations on the Importance of the American Revolution and the Means of making it a Benefit to the World." This was in 1784. And here he repeated the exultation of an earlier day : —

"With heartfelt satisfaction I see the revolution in favor of universal liberty which has taken place in America, — *a revolution which opens a new prospect in human affairs,* and begins a new era in the history of mankind.[3] . . . . Perhaps I do not go too far when I say that, next to the introduction of Christianity among mankind, the American revolution

---

[1] Page 49.   [2] Page ix.   [3] Page 2.

H

may prove the most important step in the progressive course of human improvement." [1]

Thus announcing the grandeur of the epoch, he states that it "may produce a general diffusion of the principles of humanity," and may lead mankind to see and know "that all legitimate government consists in the dominion of *equal laws*, made with common consent," which is another expression of the primal truth of the Declaration of Independence. Then, referring to the "community or confederacy" of States, he says "that it is not impossible but that by some such means *universal peace* may some time or other be produced, and all war excluded from the world"; and he asks, "Why may we not hope to see this begun in America?" [2] May America be true to this aspiration! There is also a longing for equality, and a warning against slavery, with the ejaculation, in harmony with earlier words, "Let the United States continue forever what it is now their glory to be, a confederation of States, prosperous and happy, *without lords, without bishops, and without kings*." [3] In the midst of the bloody conflict this vision had appeared, and he had sought to make it a reality.

His true friendship for our country and his devotion to humanity, with the modesty of his nature, appear in a letter to Franklin, 12th July, 1784, communicating a copy of the last production. After saying that "it is intended entirely for America," the excellent counsellor proceeds : —

"I hope the United States will forgive my presumption in supposing myself qualified to advise them. The consciousness which I have that it is well intended, and that my ad-

[1] Page 6.   [2] Page 15.   [3] Page 72.

dress to them is the effusion of a heart that wishes to serve
the best interests of society, helps to reconcile me to myself
in this instance, and it will, I hope, engage the candor of
others." [1]

The same sentiments which proved his sympathies
with our country reappeared with fresh fires at the out-
break of the French Revolution, arousing, in opposition,
the immortal eloquence of Burke. A discourse " On the
Love of Country," preached at the Old Jewry, 4th November, 1789, in commemoration of the English Revolution, with friendly glances at what was then passing
across the Channel, prompted the " Reflections on the
Revolution in France." The personal denunciation which
is the beginning of that remarkable performance is the
perpetual witness to the position of the preacher, whose
prophetic soul did not hesitate to accept the French
Revolution side by side with ours in glory and in
promise.

GOVERNOR POWNALL, 1777, 1780, 1785.

AMONG the best friends of our country abroad during
the trials of the Revolution was Thomas Pownall, called
by one biographer " a learned antiquary and politician,"
and by another " an English statesman and author."
Latterly he has so far dropped out of sight that there
are few who recognize in him either of these characters.
He was born, 1722, and died at Bath, 1805. During
this long period he held several offices. As early as
1745 he became secretary to the Commission for Trade
and Plantations. In 1753 he crossed the ocean. In
1755, as Commissioner for Massachusetts Bay, he ne-

---

[1] Franklin, Works by Sparks, Vol. X. p. 105.

gotiated with New York, New Jersey, and Pennsylvania, in union with New England, the confederated expedition against Crown Point. He was afterwards Governor of Massachusetts Bay, New Jersey, and South Carolina, successively. Returning to England, he was, in 1761, Comptroller-General of the army in Germany, with the military rank of colonel. He sat in three successive Parliaments until 1780, when he passed into private life. Hildreth gives a glimpse of his personal character, when, admitting his frank manners and liberal politics, he describes his "habits as rather freer than suited the New England standard." [1]

Pownall stands forth conspicuous for championship of our national independence, and especially for foresight with regard to our national future. In both these respects his writings are unique. Other Englishmen were in favor of independence, and saw our future also; but I doubt if any one can be named who was his equal in strenuous action or in minuteness of foresight. While the war was still proceeding, as early as 1780, he openly announced, not only that independence was inevitable, but that the new nation, "founded in nature and built up in truth," would continually expand; that its population would increase and multiply; that a civilizing activity beyond what Europe could ever know would animate it; and that its commercial and naval power would be found in every quarter of the globe. All this he set forth at length with argument and illustration, and he called his prophetic words "the *stating of the simple fact*, so little understood in the Old World." Treated at first as "unintelligible speculation" and as "unfashionable,"

[1] History of the United States, Vol. II. p. 476.

the truth he announced was neglected where it was
not rejected, but generally rejected as inadmissible, and
the author, according to his own language, "was called
by the wise men of the British Cabinet *a Wild Man,*
unfit to be employed." But these writings are a better
title now than any office. In manner they are diffuse
and pedantic; but they hardly deserve the cold judgment of John Adams, who in his old age said of them
that "a reader who has patience to search for good
sense in an uncouth and disgusting style will find in
those writings proofs of a thinking mind."[1]

He seems to have written a good deal. But the
works which will be remembered the longest are not
even mentioned by several of his biographers. Rose,
in his Biographical Dictionary, records works by him,
entitled "Antiquities of Ancient Greece"; "Roman Antiquities dug up at Bath"; "Observations on the Currents of the Ocean"; "Intellectual Physics"; and also
contributions to the Archæologia. Gorton in his Biographical Dictionary adds other titles to this list. But
neither mentions his works on America. This is another instance where the stone rejected by the builders
becomes the head of the corner.

At an early date Pownall comprehended the position
of our country, geographically. He saw the wonderful
means of internal communication supplied by its inland
waters, and also the opportunities of external commerce
supplied by the Atlantic Ocean. On the first he dwells,
in a memorial drawn up in 1756 for the Duke of Cum-
berland.[2] Nobody in our own day, after the experience
of more than a century, has portrayed more vividly

[1] Letter to William Tudor, February 4, 1817. Works, Vol. X. p. 241.
[2] Administration of the Colonies, Appendix, p. 7.

the two vast aqueous masses, — one composed of the
great lakes and their dependencies, and the other of
the Mississippi and its tributaries.   The great lakes
are described as "a wilderness of waters spreading
over the country by an infinite number and variety of
branchings, bays, and straits."   The Mississippi, with
its eastern branch, called the Ohio, is described as
having, "so far as we know, but two falls, — one at a
place called, by the French, St. Antoine, high up on
the west or main branch"; and all its waters "run
to the ocean with a still, easy, and gentle current."
The picture is completed by exhibiting the two masses
in combination : —

"The waters of each respective mass — not only the
lesser streams, but the main general body of each going
through this continent in every course and direction —
have by their approach to each other, by their communication to every quarter and in every direction, an alliance
and unity, and form one mass, or one whole." [1]

Again, depicting the intercommunication among the
several waters of the continent, and how "the watery
element claims and holds dominion over this extent
of land," he insists that all shall see these two mighty
masses in their central throne, declaring that "the great
lakes which lie upon its bosom on one hand, and the
great river Mississippi and the multitude of waters
which run into it, form there a communication, — an
alliance or dominion of the watery element, that com-
mands throughout the whole; that these great lakes
appear to be the throne, the centre of a dominion,
whose influence, by an infinite number of rivers, creeks,

---

[1] Administration of the Colonies, Appendix, p. 6.

and streams, extends itself through all and every part
of the continent, supported by the communication of,
and alliance with, the waters of the Mississippi."[1]

If these means of internal commerce were vast, those
afforded by the Atlantic Ocean were not less extensive.
The latter were developed in the volume entitled "The
Administration of the Colonies," the fourth edition of
which, published in 1768, is now before me. This was
after the differences between the Colonies and the
mother country had begun, but before the idea of
independence had shown itself. Pownall insisted that
the Colonies ought to be considered as parts of the
realm, entitled to representation in Parliament. This
was a constitutional unity. But he portrayed a commercial unity also, which he represented in attractive
forms. The British Isles, and the British possessions
in the Atlantic and in America, were, according to him,
"one grand marine dominion," and ought, therefore, by
policy, to be united into one empire, with one centre.
On this he dwells at length, and the picture is presented repeatedly.[2] It was incident to the crisis in
the world produced by the predominance of the commercial spirit already beginning to rule the powers of
Europe. It was the duty of England to place herself
at the head of this great movement.

"As the rising of this crisis forms precisely the *object*
on which government should be employed, so the taking
leading measures towards the forming all those Atlantic
and American possessions into one empire, of which Great
Britain should be the commercial and political centre, is
the *precise duty* of government at this crisis."

1 Administration of the Colonies, p. 9.
2 Ibid., pp. 9, 10, 164.

This was his desire. But he saw clearly the resources as well as the rights of the Colonies, and was satisfied that, if power were not consolidated under the constitutional auspices of England, it would be transferred to the other side of the Atlantic. Here his words are prophetic: —

"The whole train of events, the whole course of business, must perpetually bring forward into practice, and necessarily in the end into establishment, *either an American or a British union*. There is no other alternative."

The necessity for union is enforced in a manner which foreshadows our national Union: —

"The Colonial Legislature does not answer all purposes; is incompetent and inadequate to many purposes. Something more is necessary, — *either a common union among themselves*, or a common union of subordination under the one general legislature of the state."[1]

Then, again, in another place of the same work, after representing the declarations of power over the Colonies as little better than mockery, he prophesies: —

"Such is the actual state of the really existing system of our dominions, that *neither the power of government over these various parts can long continue under the present mode of administration*, nor the great interests of commerce extended throughout the whole long subsist under the present system of the laws of trade."[2]

Recent events may give present interest to his views, in this same work, on the nature and necessity of a paper currency, where he follows Franklin. The prin-

[1] Administration of the Colonies, p. 165.
[2] Ibid., p. 16.

cipal points of his plan were, that bills of credit, to a
certain amount, should be printed in England for the
use of the Colonies; that a loan-office should be established in each Colony to issue bills, take securities, and
receive the payment; that the bills should be issued
for ten years, bearing interest at five per cent, — one
tenth part of the sum borrowed to be paid annually,
with interest; and that they should be a legal tender.

When the differences had flamed forth in war, then
the prophet became more earnest. His utterances
deserve to be rescued from oblivion. He was open,
almost defiant. As early as 2d December, 1777, some
months before our treaty with France, he declared,
from his place in Parliament, "that the sovereignty
of this country over America is abolished and gone
forever"; "that they are determined at all events to
be independent, *and will be so*"; and "that all the
treaty this country can ever expect with America is
federal, and that, probably, only commercial." In this
spirit he said to the House: —

"Until you shall be convinced that you are no longer
sovereigns over America, but that the United States are
an independent, sovereign people, — until you are prepared
to treat with them as such, — it is of no consequence at
all what schemes or plans of conciliation this side of the
House or that may adopt."[1]

The position taken in Parliament he maintained by
writings, and here he depicted the great destinies of
our country. He began with "A Memorial to the
Sovereigns of Europe," published early in 1780, and
afterwards, through the influence of John Adams,

[1] Parliamentary History, Vol. XIX. pp. 527, 528. See also p. 1137.

while at the Hague, abridged and translated into French. In this remarkable production independence was the least that he claimed for us. Thus he foretells our future : —

"North America is become a new primary planet in the system of the world, which, while it takes its own course, must have effect on the orbit of every other planet, and shift the common centre of gravity of the whole system of the European world. North America is *de facto* an independent power, which has taken its equal station with other powers, and must be so *de jure*. . . . . The independence of America is fixed as fate. She is mistress of her own future, knows that she is so, and will actuate that power which she feels she hath, so as to establish her own system *and to change the system of Europe.*" [1]

Not only is the new power to take an independent place, but it is "to change the system of Europe." For all this its people are amply prepared. "Standing on that high ground of improvement up to which the most enlightened parts of Europe have advanced, like eaglets, they commence the first efforts of their pinions from a towering advantage." [2]   This same conviction appears in another form : —

"North America has advanced, and is every day advancing, to growth of state, with a steady and continually accelerating motion, of which there has never yet been any example in Europe.[3] . . . . It is a vitality, liable to many disorders, many dangerous diseases ; but it is young and strong, and will struggle, by the vigor of internal healing principles of life, against those evils, and surmount them. Its strength will grow with its years." [4]

---

[1] Memorial to the Sovereigns of Europe, pp. 4, 5.
[2] Ibid., p. 43.   [3] Ibid., p. 56.   [4] Ibid., p. 69.

He then dwells in detail on "the progressive population" here; on our advantage in being "on the other side of the globe, where there is no enemy"; on the products of the soil, among which is "bread-corn to a degree that has wrought it to a staple export for the supply of the Old World"; on the fisheries, which he calls "mines of more solid riches than all the silver of Potosi"; on the inventive spirit of the people; and on their commercial activity. Of such a people it is easy to predict great things; and our prophet announces, —

1. That the new state will be "an active naval power," exercising a peculiar influence on commerce, and, through commerce, on the political system of the Old World, — becoming the arbitress of commerce, and, perhaps, the mediatrix of peace.[1]

2. That shipbuilding and the science of navigation have made such progress in America that her people will be able to build and navigate cheaper than any country in Europe, even Holland, with all her economy.[2]

3. That the peculiar articles to be had from America only, and so much sought in Europe, must give Americans a preference in those markets.[3]

4. That a people "whose empire stands singly predominant on a great continent" can hardly "suffer in their borders such a monopoly as the European Hudson Bay Company"; that it cannot be stopped by Cape Horn or the Cape of Good Hope; that before long they will be found "trading in the South Sea and in China"; and that the Dutch "will hear of them in the Spice Islands."[4]

[1] Memorial to the Sovereigns of Europe, pp. 74, 77.
[2] Ibid., p. 82.   [3] Ibid., p. 83.   [4] Ibid., p. 85.

5. That by constant intercommunion of business and correspondence, and by increased knowledge with regard to the ocean, "America will seem every day to approach nearer and nearer to Europe"; that the old alarm at the sea will subside, and "a thousand attractive motives will become the irresistible cause of *an almost general emigration to the New World*"; and that "many of the most useful, enterprising spirits, and much of the active property, will go there also."[1]

6. That "North America will become a *free port* to all the nations of the world indiscriminately, and will expect, insist on, and demand, in fair reciprocity, a *free market* in all those nations with whom she trades"; and that, adhering to this principle, she must be, "in the course of time, the chief carrier of the commerce of the whole world."[2]

7. That America must avoid complication with European politics, or "the entanglement of alliances, having no connections with Europe other than commercial";[3]—all of which at a later day was put forth by Washington in his Farewell Address when he said: "The great rule of conduct for us, in regard to foreign nations, is, in extending our commercial relations, to have with them as little political concern as possible"; and also when he said: "Why, by interweaving our destiny with that of any part of Europe, entangle our peace and prosperity in the toils of European ambition, rivalship, interest, humor, or caprice?"[4]

8. That similar modes of living and thinking, the same manners and same fashions, the same language

<hr/>

[1] Memorial to the Sovereigns of Europe, p. 87.
[2] Ibid., pp. 60, 97.
[3] Ibid., p. 78.
[4] Writings by Sparks, Vol. XII. pp. 231, 232.

and old habits of national love, impressed on the heart and not yet effaced, *the very indentings of the fracture where North America is broken off from England, all conspire naturally to a rejuncture by alliance.*[1]

9. That the sovereigns of Europe, "who have despised the unfashioned, awkward youth of America," and have neglected to interweave their interests with the rising States, when they find the system of the new empire not only obstructing, but superseding, the old system of Europe, and crossing all their settled maxims, will call upon their ministers and wise men, "Come, curse me this people, for they are too mighty for me."[2]

This remarkable appeal was followed by two memorials, "drawn up solely for the king's use, and designed solely for his eye," dated at Richmond, January, 1782, where the author most persuasively urges his Majesty to treat with the Colonies on the footing of independence, and with this view to institute a preliminary negotiation "as with free states *de facto* under a truce." And on the signature of the treaty of peace he wrote a private letter to Franklin, dated at Richmond, 28th February, 1783, where he testifies again to the magnitude of the event: —

"MY OLD FRIEND, — I write this to congratulate you on the establishment of your country as a free and sovereign power, taking its equal station amongst the powers of the world. I congratulate you, in particular, as chosen by Providence to be a principal instrument in this great Revolution, — *a Revolution that has stranger marks of Divine interposition, superseding the ordinary course of human affairs, than any other event which this world has experienced.*"

1 Memorial to the Sovereigns of Europe, p. 93.
2 Ibid., p. 91.

The prophet closes his letter by allusion to a proposed tour of America, adding that, "if there ever was an object worth travelling to see, and worthy of the contemplation of a philosopher, it is that in which he may see the beginning of a great empire at its foundation."[1] He communicated this purpose also to John Adams, who answered him that "he would be received respectfully in every part of America, that he had always been considered friendly to America, and that his writings had been useful to our cause."[2]

Then came another word, first published in 1783, entitled "A Memorial addressed to the Sovereigns of America, by Governor Pownall," of which he gave the mistaken judgment to a private friend, that it was "the best thing he ever wrote." Here for the first time American citizens are called "sovereigns." At the beginning he explains and indicates the simplicity with which he addresses them : —

"Having presumed to address to the Sovereigns of Europe a Memorial . . . . permit me now to address this Memorial to you, Sovereigns of America. I shall not address you with the court titles of Gothic Europe, nor with those of servile Asia. I will neither address your Sublimity or Majesty, your Grace or Holiness, your Eminence or High-mightiness, your Excellence or Honors. What are titles where things themselves are known and understood ? What title did the Republic of Rome take ? The state was known to be sovereign and the citizens to be free. What could add to this ? Therefore, United States and Citizens of America, I address you as you are."[3]

1 Franklin, Works by Sparks, Vol. IX. p. 491.
2 John Adams, Works, Vol. VIII. p. 179.
3 Memorial to the Sovereigns of America, pp. 5, 6.

Here again are the same constant sympathy with liberty, the same confidence in our national destinies, and the same aspirations for our prosperity, mingled with warnings against disturbing influences. He exhorts that all our foundations should be "laid in nature"; that there should be "no contention for, nor acquisition of, unequal domination in men"; and that union should be established on the attractive principle by which all are drawn to a common centre. He fears difficulty in making the line of frontier between us and the British Provinces "a line of peace," as it ought to be; he is anxious lest something may break out between us and Spain; and he suggests that possibly, "in the cool hours of unimpassioned reflection," we may learn the danger of our "alliances," — referring plainly to that original alliance with France which, at a later day, was the occasion of such trouble. Two other warnings occur. One is against Slavery, which is more memorable, because in an earlier memorial he enumerates among articles of commerce "African slaves carried by a circuitous trade in American shipping to the West India market."[1] The other warning is thus strongly expressed: "Every inhabitant of America is, *de facto* as well as *de jure*, equal, in his essential, inseparable rights of the individual, to any other individual, and is, in these rights, independent of any power that any other can assume over him, over his labor, or his property. This is a principle in act and deed, and not a mere speculative theorem."[2]

This strange and striking testimony, all from one man, is enhanced by his farewell words to Franklin. As

---

[1] Memorial to the Sovereigns of Europe, p. 83.
[2] Memorial to the Sovereigns of America, p. 55.

Pownall heard that the great philosopher and negotiator was about to embark for the United States, he wrote to him from Lausanne, 3d July, 1785 : —

"Adieu, my dear friend. You are going to a New World, formed to exhibit a scene which the Old World never yet saw. You leave me here in the Old World, which, like myself, begins to feel, as Asia hath felt, that it is wearing out apace. We shall never meet again on this earth ; but there is another world where we shall, and *where we shall be understood.*"

The correspondence was continued across the intervening ocean. In a letter to Franklin, dated at Bristol, 8th April, 1788, the same devoted reformer refers to the Congress at Albany in 1754, "when the events, which have since come into fact, first began to develop themselves, as ready to burst into bloom and to bring forth the fruits of liberty which you at present enjoy." He is cheered in his old age by the proceedings in the convention to frame a constitution with Franklin's "report of a system of sovereignty founded in law and above which law only was sovereign," and he begins "to entertain hopes for the liberties of America, and for what will be an asylum one day or other to a remnant of mankind who wish and deserve to live with political liberty." His disturbance at the Presidential term breaks out : "I have some fears of mischief from the *orbit of four years'* period, which you give to the rotation of the office of President. It may become the ground of intrigue."[1] Here friendly anxiety is elevated by hope where America appears as the asylum of Liberty.

[1] Franklin, Works, Vol. X. pp. 343, 344.

Clearly Pownall was not understood in his time ; but it is evident that he understood our country as few Englishmen since have been able to understand it.

How few of his contemporaries saw America with his insight and courage! The prevailing sentiment was typified in the conduct of George III., so boldly arraigned in the Declaration of Independence. Individual opinions also attest the contrast and help to glorify Pownall. Thus Shirley, like himself a Massachusetts governor, in advising the King to strengthen Louisburg, wrote, under date of July 10, 1745 : —

"It would, by its vicinity to the British colonies, and being the key of 'em, give the crown of Great Britain a most absolute hold and command of 'em, if ever there should come a time when they should go restiff and disposed to shake off their dependency upon their mother country, *the possibility of which seems some centuries further off than it does to some gentlemen at home.*" [1]

Nothing of the prophet here. *Nor* was Hume more penetrating in his History first published, although he commemorates properly the early settlement of the country : —

"What chiefly renders the reign of James memorable is the commencement of the English colonies in America; colonies established on the noblest footing that has been known in any age or nation. . . . .

"Speculative reasoning during that age raised many objections to the planting of those remote colonies, and foretold that, after draining their mother country of inhabitants, they would soon shake off their yoke and erect an independent government in America ; but time has shown that the

1 Palfrey, Compendious History of New England, 1728–65.

6 *   I

views entertained by those who encouraged such generous undertakings were more just and solid. *A mild government and great moral force have preserved and may still preserve during some time the dominion of England over her colonies.*" [1]

In making the reign of James chiefly memorable by the colonies, the eminent historian shows a just appreciation of events; but he seems to have written hastily, and rather from imagination than evidence, when he announces contemporary prophecy, "that, after draining their mother country of inhabitants, they would soon shake off their yoke and erect an independent government in America," and is plainly without prophetic instinct with regard to "the dominion of England over her colonies."

CÉRISIER, 1778, 1780.

AGAIN a Frenchman appears on our list, Antoine Marie Cérisier, who was born at Chatillon in the Bresse, 1749, and died at Paris, 1st July, 1828, after a checkered existence. Being Secretary of the French Legation at the Hague, he early became interested in the history of Holland and her heroic struggle for independence. An elaborate work in ten volumes on the "General History of the United Provinces," [2] appearing first in French and afterwards translated into Dutch, attests his industry and zeal, and down to this day is accepted as the best in French literature on this interesting subject. Naturally the historian of the mighty effort to overthrow the domination of Spain sympathized with the kindred effort in America. In a series of works he bore his testimony to our cause.

[1] History of England. Appendix to Reign of James I.
[2] Works, Vol. VII. pp. 589, 590.

John Adams was received at the Hague as American Minister, 19th April, 1782. In his despatch to the Continental Congress, 16th May, 1782, he wrote : "How shall I mention another gentleman, whose name, perhaps, Congress never heard, but who, in my opinion, has done more decided and essential service to the American cause and reputation within these last eighteen months, than any other man in Europe." Then, after describing him as "beyond all contradiction one of the greatest historians and political characters in Europe, ... possessed of the most generous principles and sentiments of liberty, and exceedingly devoted by principle and affection to the American cause," our Minister announces : "His pen has erected a monument to the American cause more glorious and more durable than brass or marble. His writings have been read like oracles, and his sentiments weekly echoed and re-echoed in gazettes and pamphlets."[1] And yet these have passed out of sight.

First in time was an elaborate work in French, purporting to be translated from the English, which appeared at Utrecht in 1778, entitled, "History of the Foundation of the Ancient Republics adapted to the present Dispute of Great Britain with the American Colonies." Learning and philosophy were elevated by visions of the future. With the representation of the Colonies in Parliament, he foresees the time when "the influence of America will become preponderant in Parliament, and *can, perhaps, transport the seat of empire* to their country, and so, without danger and without

---

[1] Histoire de la Fondation des Anciennes Républiques adaptée à la dispute présente de la Grande Bretagne avec les Colonies Américaines. Utrecht, 1778.

convulsive agitation, render this immense continent, already so favored by nature, the theatre of one of the greatest and freest governments which ever existed." [1] Then, indulging in another vision, where French emigrants and Canadians, already invited to enter the Confederacy, mingle with English colonists, he beholds at the head of the happy settlements "men known for their superior genius and their enthusiasm for liberty," and he catches the strains of ancient dramatists, "whose masterpieces will breathe and inspire the hatred of tyrants and despots." Then touching a practical point in government, he exclaims: "The human species will not be degraded, outraged by that odious and barbarous distinction of nobles and plebeians, as if anybody could be more or less than a man." And then again, "Could not that admirable democracy which I have so often pleased myself in tracing be established there?" [2]

This was followed in the same year by another publication, also in French, entitled "Impartial Observations of a True Dutchman, in Answer to the Address of a self-styled Good Dutchman to his Countrymen." [3] Here there is no longer question of colonial representation in Parliament, or of British empire transported to America, but of separation, with its lofty future: —

"This revolution is then the most happy event which could arrive to the human species and to all the States separately. In fine, sensitive souls see with transport that the crime of those who have discovered and devastated this

1 Page 155.
2 Page 176.
3 Observations Impartiales d'un Vrai Hollandois pour servir de Réponse au Discours d'un soi-disant Bon Hollandois à ses Compatriotes. Amsterdam, 1778.

immense continent is at last to be repaired, and recognize the United States of North America as replacing the numerous nations which European cruelty has caused to disappear from Southern America." [1]

Then, addressing Englishmen directly, the Frenchman thus counsels : —

"Englishmen ! it is necessary for you to submit to your destiny, and renounce people who do not wish longer to recognize you. To avoid giving them any anxiety, and to prevent all dispute in the future, *have the courage to abandon to them the surrounding countries which have not yet thrown off your yoke. . . . . Let Canada make a fourteenth confederate State.* What glory for you to have labored first for this interesting revolution ! What glory for you that these settlements, derived from your bosom, are associated with a powerful confederation, and govern themselves as a Republic !"

The idea of Canada as a "fourteenth confederate State" was in unison with the aspiration and invitation of the Continental Congress.

Another friendly work in French, pretending to be from the English, saw the light in 1780, and is entitled "The Destiny of America; or, Pictorial Dialogues." [2] Among the parties to the colloquies are Lord North, with other English personages, and a Philosopher, who must be the author. Among the topics considered are the causes of pending events, the policy of European powers relative to the war, and the influence it must have on the happiness of the Human Family. In answer to Lord North, who asks the precious means to

[1] Page 15.
[2] Le Destin de l'Amérique ou Dialogues Pittoresques. Londres (Hollande), 1780.

save honor and welfare, the Philosopher replies : " Commence by proclaiming the independence of the thirteen revolted Colonies, of Florida, *and of Canada*, and then, in a manner not less solemn, renounce Jamaica, Barbadoes, and all the Windward Isles." [1] This is to be followed by the freedom of the Spanish and French colonies, — also of the Dutch, the Portuguese, and the Danish. Then, rising in aspiration, the Philosopher, exalting the good of humanity over that of any nation, proclaims that the root of future wars must be destroyed, that the ocean may not be reddened with blood ; but this destiny will be prolonged "if America does not become entirely free." [2] Then, looking forward to the time when nations will dispute on the ocean only in commercial activity, and man will cease to be the greatest enemy of man, he declares : " If Universal Peace could be more than the dream of good men, what event could accelerate it more than the independence of the two Americas ? " [3] Confessing that he does not expect the applause of the present age, he concludes, " My heart tells me that I shall have the support of all free and sympathetic souls, and the suffrage of posterity." [4] Most surely he has mine. Nothing can be happier than the thought that Universal Peace would be accelerated by American freedom, thus enhancing even this great boon.

SIR WILLIAM JONES, 1781.

I AM glad to enter upon our list the name of this illustrious scholar, who was born in London, 28th September, 1746, and died in India, 24th April, 1794.

[1] Page 109.
[2] Page 115.
[3] Page 113.
[4] Page 112.

If others have excelled Sir William Jones in different departments of human activity, no Englishman has attained equal eminence in so many, and at the same time borne the priceless crown of character. His wonderful attainments and his various genius excite admiration, but his goodness awakens love. It is pleasant to know that his benediction rests upon our country.

From boyhood to his last breath he was always industrious, thus helping the generous gifts of nature, — and it is not easy to say where he was most eminent. As a jurist he is memorable for the " Essay on the Law of Bailments," undoubtedly at the time it appeared the most complete and beautiful contribution to the science of jurisprudence in the English language. As a judge, he was the voice of the law and of justice, so that his appointment to a high judicial station in India was called " the greatest blessing ever conferred by the British Government on the inhabitants of the East." [1] As a linguist, knowing no less than twenty-eight languages, he was the predecessor of Sir William Humboldt and the less scholarly prodigy, Mezzofante, while as a philologist he will find a parallel in the former rather than the latter. As an Orientalist, he was not only the first of his time, but the pioneer through whom the literature of the East was opened to European study and curiosity. As a poet, he is enshrined forever by his Ode, modestly called " in imitation of Alcæus," [2] and doubtless inspired by sympathy with the American cause.

" What constitutes a State?
Not high-raised battlement on labored mound,
Thick wall or moated gate;
NO; men, high-minded men,

[1] Meadley's Memoirs of Paley, p. 221.
[2] Dated Abergavenny, March 31, 1781.

Men, who their duties know
But know their rights, and, knowing, dare maintain;
Prevent the long-aimed blow,
And crush the tyrant while they rend the chain; —
These constitute a State."

To all these accomplishments add the glowing emotions of his noble nature, his love of virtue, his devotion to freedom, his sympathy for the poor and downtrodden. His biographer records as "a favorite opinion of Sir William Jones, that all men are born with *an equal capacity for improvement*,"[1] and also reports him as saying, "I see clearly under the sun the two classes of men whom Solomon describes, the oppressor and the oppressed. . . . . I shall cultivate my fields and think as little as possible of monarchs or oligarchs."[2] With these declarations it is easy to credit Dr. Paley, who said of him, "He was a great republican when I knew him."[3] Like seeks like, and a long intimacy in the family of the good Bishop of St. Asaph, ending in a happy marriage with his eldest daughter, shows how he must have sympathized with the American cause and with the future of our country.

Our author had been the tutor of Lord Althorp, the same who, as Earl Spencer, became so famous a bibliophile and a patron of Dibdin, and on the marriage of his pupil with Miss Lavinia Brigham, he was moved to commemorate it in a poem, entitled "The Muse Recalled; an Ode on the Nuptials of Lord Viscount Althorp and Miss Lavinia Brigham, eldest Daughter of Charles Lord Lucon, March 6, 1781," which his critic, Wraxall, calls "one of the most beautiful lyric productions in the

---

1 Teignmouth's Life of Sir William Jones, p. 406.
2 Ibid., p. 365.
3 Meadley's Memoirs of Paley, p. 221.

English language, emulating at once the fame of Milton and of Gray."[1]   But beyond the strain of personal sympathy, congenial to the occasion, was a passion for America, and the prophetic spirit which belongs to the poet. After lamenting that "freedom and concord repudiate the sons of Albion," all the virtues disappear.

> "Truth, Justice, Reason, Valor, with them fly,
> To seek a purer soil, a more congenial sky."

But the soil and sky which they seek are of the Delaware : —

> "Beyond the vast Atlantic deep
> A dome by viewless genii shall be raised,
> The walls of adamant, compact and steep,
> The portals with sky-tinctured gems emblazed.
> There, on a lofty throne shall Virtue stand;
> To her the youth of Delaware shall kneel;
> And when her smiles rain plenty o'er the land,
> Bow, tyrants, bow beneath the 'avenging steel.'
> *Commerce with fleets shall mock the waves,*
> *And arts that flourish not with slaves,*
> *Dancing with every Grace and Muse,*
> *Shall bid the valleys laugh and heavenly beams diffuse.*"

Wraxall complains,[2] that here, in a fine frenzy of inspiration, the poet seems to behold, as in a vision, Washington and Congress exulting in the overthrow of all subjection to Great Britain, while George III. is pretty clearly designated in the apostrophe to tyrants. But to an American the most captivating verses are those which open the vista of peaceful triumphs where commerce and the arts unite with every Grace and every Muse.

Kindred in sentiment were other contemporary verses by the anonymous author of the " Heroic Epistle to Sir

[1] Historical Memoirs of his own Time, Vol. II. p. 378, March, 1781 (ed. London, 1836).
[2] Ibid., p. 379.

William Chambers," now understood to be the poet
Mason,[1] which Wraxall praises for their beauty, but
condemns for their politics.[2] After describing the corruption of the House of Commons under Lord North,
the poet declares that it will augment in enormity and
profligacy, —

> " Till, mocked and jaded with the puppet play,
> Old England's genius turns with scorn away,
> Ascends his sacred bark, the sails unfurl'd,
> *And steers his State to the wide Western World.*
> High on the helm majestic Freedom stands,
> In act of cold contempt she waves her hands;
> Take, slaves, she cries, the realms that I disown,
> Renounce your birthright and destroy my throne!"

The two poets united in a common cause. One transported to the other side of the Atlantic the virtues
which had been the glory of Britain, and the other carried there nothing less than the sovereign genius of the
great nation itself.

COUNT ARANDA, 1783.

THE Count Aranda was one of the first of Spanish
statesmen and diplomatists, and one of the richest subjects of Spain in his day; born at Saragossa, 1718, and
died 1799. He, too, is one of our prophets. Originally
a soldier, he became ambassador, governor of a province,
and prime minister. In the latter post he displayed
character as well as ability, and was the benefactor of
his country. He drove the Jesuits from Spain and
dared to oppose the Inquisition. He was a philosopher, and, like Pope Benedict XIV., corresponded with
Voltaire. Such a liberal spirit was out of place in

---

[1] Walpole's Last Journals, Vol. I. p. 187, March, 1773.
[2] Historical Memoirs, Vol. II. p. 77, March, 1781.

Spain. Compelled to resign in 1773, he found a retreat at Paris as ambassador, where he came into communication with Franklin, Adams, and Jay, and finally signed the Treaty of Paris, by which Spain acknowledged our independence. Shortly afterwards he returned to Spain and took the place of Florida Blanca as prime minister. He was emphatically a statesman, and as such did not hesitate to take responsibility even contrary to express orders. An instance of this civic courage was when, for the sake of peace between Spain and England, he accepted the Floridas instead of Gibraltar, on which the eminent French publicist, M. Rayneval, remarks that "history furnishes few examples of such a character and such loyalty." [1]

Franklin, on meeting him, records, in his letter to the secret committee of Congress, that he seemed "well disposed to us." [2] Shortly afterwards he had another interview with him, which he thus chronicles in his journal : —

"*Saturday, June 29th* [1782]. — We went together to the Spanish Ambassador's, who received us with great civility and politeness. He spoke with Mr. Jay on the subject of the treaty they were to make together. . . . . On our going out, he took pains himself to open the folding-doors for us, which is a high compliment here, and told us he would return our visit (*rendre son devoir*), and then fix a day with us for dining with him." [3]

Adams, in his journal, describes a Sunday dinner at his house, then a " new building in the finest situation of Paris," [4] being part of the incomparable palace, with

1 Institutions du Droit de la Nature et des Gens, Tom. II. p. 311.
2 Works, Vol VIII. p. 194.
3 Works, Vol. IX. p. 350.
4 Works, Vol. III. p. 379.

its columnar front, still admired as it looks on the Place
de la Concorde. Jay also describes a dinner with the
Count, who was "living in great splendor, with an assort-
ment of wines the finest in Europe," and was "the ablest
Spaniard he had ever known"; showing by his conversation "that his court is in earnest," and appearing "frank
and candid, as well as sagacious." [1] These hospitalities
have a peculiar interest, when it is known, as it now is,
that Count Aranda regarded the acknowledgment of our
independence with "grief and dread." But these sentiments were disguised from our ministers.

After signing the Treaty of Paris, by which Spain
acknowledged our independence, Aranda addressed a
memoir secretly to King Charles III., in which his
opinions on this event are set forth. This prophetic
document slumbered for a long time in the confidential
archives of the Spanish crown. Coxe, in his "Memoirs
of the House of Bourbon in Spain," which are founded
on a rare collection of original documents, makes no
allusion to it. The memoir appears for the first time
in a volume published at Paris in 1837, and entitled
"*Gouvernement de Charles III., Roi d'Espagne, ou Instruction réservée à la Junte d'État par ce Monarque.
Publié par D. André Muriel.*" The editor had translated
into French the Memoirs of Coxe, and was probably led
by this labor to make the supplementary collection. An
abstract of the memoir of Aranda appears in one of the
historical dissertations of the Mexican authority, Alaman, who said of it that it has "a just celebrity, because
results have made it pass for a prophecy." [2] I translate
it now from the French of Muriel.

---

[1] William Jay, Life of John Jay, Vol. I. p. 140 ; Vol. II. p. 101.
[2] Dissertaciones sobre la Historia de la Republica Megicana, Tom. III. pp.
351, 352.

"Memoir communicated secretly to the King by his Excellency the Count Aranda, on the Independence of the English Colonies, after having signed the Treaty of Paris of 1783.

" The independence of the English colonies has been acknowledged. This is for me an occasion of grief and dread. France has few possessions in America ; but she should have considered that Spain, her intimate ally, has many, and that she is left to-day exposed to terrible shocks. From the beginning, France has acted contrary to her true interests in encouraging and seconding this independence ; I have so declared often to the ministers of this nation. What could happen better for France than to see the English and the colonists destroy each other in a party warfare which could only augment her power and favor her interests ? The antipathy which reigns between France and England blinded the French Cabinet ; it forgot that its interest consisted in remaining a tranquil spectator of this conflict ; and, once launched in the arena, it dragged us unhappily, and by virtue of the family compact, into a war entirely contrary to our proper interest.

" I will not stop here to examine the opinions of some statesmen, our own countrymen as well as foreigners, which I share, on *the difficulty of preserving our power in America. Never have so extensive possessions, placed at a great distance from the metropolis, been long preserved.* To this cause, applicable to all colonies, must be added others peculiar to the Spanish possessions ; namely, the difficulty of succoring them in case of need ; the vexations to which the unhappy inhabitants have been exposed from some of the governors ; the distance of the supreme authority to which they must have recourse for the redress of grievances, which causes years to pass before justice is done to their complaints ; the vengeance of the local authorities to which they continue exposed while waiting ; the difficulty of knowing the truth at so great a distance ; finally, the means which the viceroys and governors, from being Spaniards, cannot fail to have for obtaining favorable judgments in Spain; all these different circumstances will render the inhabitants of America discontented, and make them attempt efforts to obtain independence as soon as they shall have a propitious occasion.

"Without entering into any of these considerations, I shall confine myself now to that which occupies us from the dread of seeing ourselves exposed to dangers from the new power which we have just recognized in a country where there is no other in condition to arrest its progress. *This Federal Republic is born a pygmy*, so to speak. It required the support and the forces of two powers as great as Spain and France in order to attain independence. *A day will come when it will be a giant, even a colossus formidable in these countries.* It will then forget the benefits which it has received from the two powers, and will dream of nothing but to organize itself. *Liberty of conscience, the facility for establishing a new population on immense lands, as well as the advantages of the new government, will draw thither agriculturists and artisans from all the nations; for men always run after fortune. And in a few years we shall see with true grief the tyrannical existence of this same colossus of which I speak.*

"The first movement of this power, when it has arrived at its aggrandizement, will be to obtain possession of the Floridas, in order to dominate the Gulf of Mexico. After having rendered commerce with New Spain difficult for us, it will aspire to the conquest of this vast empire, which it will not be possible for us to defend against a formidable power established on the same continent, and in its neighborhood. These fears are well founded, Sire; they will be changed into reality in a few years, if, indeed, there are not other disorders in our Americas still more fatal. This observation is justified by what has happened in all ages, and with all nations which have begun to rise. Man is the same every-

where; the difference of climate does not change the nature
of our sentiments; he who finds the opportunity of acquiring
power and of aggrandizing himself, profits by it always. How
then can we expect the Americans to respect the kingdom of
New Spain, when they shall have the facility of possessing
themselves of this rich and beautiful country? A wise policy
counsels us to take precautions against evils which may happen. This thought has occupied my whole mind, since, as
Minister Plenipotentiary of your Majesty, and conformably
to your royal will and instructions, I signed the Peace of
Paris. I have considered this important affair with all the
attention of which I am capable, and after much reflection
drawn from the knowledge, military as well as political,
which I have been able to acquire in my long career, I think
that, in order to escape the great losses with which we are
threatened, there remains nothing but the means which I am
about to have the honor of exhibiting to your Majesty.

"Your Majesty must relieve yourself of all your possessions on the continent of the two Americas, *preserving only
the islands of Cuba and Porto Rico* in the northern part, and
some other convenient one in the southern part, to serve as
a seaport or trading-place for Spanish commerce.

"In order to accomplish this great thought in a manner
becoming to Spain, three infants must be placed in America,
— one as king of Mexico, another as king of Peru, and the
third as king of the Terra Firma. Your Majesty will take
the title of Emperor."

I have sometimes heard this remarkable memoir
called apocryphal, but without reason, except because
its foresight is so remarkable. The Mexican historian
Alaman treats it as genuine, and, after praising it, in-
forms us that the proposition of Count Aranda to the
king was not taken into consideration, which, according
to him, was "disastrous to all, and especially to the peo-

ple of America, who in this way would have obtained independence without struggle or anarchy.[1]   Meanwhile all the American possessions of the Spanish crown, except Cuba and Porto Rico, have become independent, as predicted, and the new power, known as the United States, which at that time was a "pygmy," is a "colossus."

In proposing a throne for Spanish America, Aranda was preceded by no less a person than the great French engineer and fort-builder, Marshal Vauban, who, during the reverses of the war of the Spanish Succession, submitted to the court of France that Philip the Fifth should be sent to reign in America, and the king is said to have consented.[2]

Aranda was not alone in surprise at the course of Spain.   The English traveller Burnaby, in his edition of 1796, mentions this as one of the reasons for the success of the Colonists, and declares that he had not supposed, originally, "that Spain would join in a plan inevitably leading by slow and imperceptible steps to the final loss of all her rich possessions in America."[3] This was not an uncommon idea.   The same anxieties appeared in one of Mr. Adams's Dutch correspondents, whose report of fearful prophecies has been already mentioned.[4]   John Adams also records in his diary, under date of 14th December, 1779, on landing at Ferrol in Spain, that, according to the report of various persons, "the Spanish nation in general have been of opinion that the Revolution in America was of bad example

[1] Alaman, Disertaciones, Tom. III. p 333.
[2] Voltaire, Siècle de Louis XIV., Chap. XXI. : Œuvres, Tom. XXIII. p. 336 (ed. 1785).
[3] Travels in North America, Preface, p. 10.
[4] *Ante*, pp. 56 – 58.

to the Spanish colonies, and dangerous to the interests of Spain, as the United States, should they become ambitious, and be seized with the spirit of conquest, might aim at Mexico and Peru."[1] All this is entirely in harmony with the memoir of the Spanish statesman.

WILLIAM PALEY, 1785.

WITH the success of the American Revolution prophecy entered other spheres, and here we welcome a remarkable writer, the Rev. William Paley, an English divine, who was born July, 1743, and died 25th May, 1805. He is known for various works of great contemporary repute, all commended by a style of singular transparency and admirably adapted to the level of opinion at the time. If they are gradually vanishing from sight, it is because other works, especially in philosophy, are more satisfactory and touch higher chords.

His earliest considerable work, and for a long period a popular text-book of education, was the well-known "Principles of Moral and Political Philosophy," which first appeared in 1785. Here, with grave errors and a reprehensible laxity on certain topics, he did much for truth. The clear vision with which he saw the enormity of slavery was not disturbed by any prevailing interest at home, and he constantly testified against it. American Independence furnished occasion for a prophetic aspiration of more than common value, because embodied in a work of morals especially for the young.

"The great revolution which has taken place in the Western World may probably conduce (and who knows but that it was designed?) *to accelerate the fall of this abominable*

---

[1] Works, Vol. III. p. 234.

tyranny; and now that this contest, and the passions which attend it, are no more, there may succeed perhaps a season for reflecting, whether a legislature, which had so long lent its assistance to the support of an institution replete with human misery, was fit to be trusted with an empire the most extensive that ever obtained in any age or quarter of the world." [1]

In thus associating Emancipation with American Independence, the philosopher became an unconscious associate of Lafayette, who, on the consummation of peace, invited Washington to this beneficent enterprise, alas! in vain.[2]

Paley did not confine his testimony to the pages of philosophy, but openly united with the Abolitionists of the day. To help the movement against the slave-trade, he encountered the *claim of pecuniary compensation* for the partakers in the traffic, by a brief essay, in 1789, entitled "Arguments against the unjust Pretensions of Slave Dealers and Holders to be indemnified by pecuniary Allowances at the public Expense, in Case the Slave-Trade should be abolished." [3] This was sent to the Abolition Committee, by whom the substance was presented to the public; but unhappily the essay was lost or mislaid.

His honorable interest in the cause was attested by a speech at a public meeting of the inhabitants of Carlisle, over which he presided, 9th February, 1792. Here he denounced the slave-trade as that "diabolical traffic," and by a plain similitude, as applicable to slavery as to the trade in slaves, held it up to judgment: —

1 Moral and Political Philosophy, Book III. Part 2, Chap. 3: "Slavery."
2 Correspondence of the American Revolution: Letters to Washington (ed. Sparks), Vol. III. p. 547.
3 Meadley, Memoirs of Paley, p. 151.

" None will surely plead in favor of scalping. But suppose scalps should become of request in Europe, and a trade in them be carried on with the American Indians, might it not be justly said that the Europeans, by their trade in scalps, did all they could to perpetuate among the natives of America the inhuman practice of scalping ? " [1]

Strange that the philosopher who extenuated duelling should have been so true and lofty against slavery. For this at least he deserves our grateful praise.

BURNS, 1788.

FROM Count Aranda to Robert Burns, — from the rich and titled minister, faring sumptuously in the best house of Paris, to the poor ploughboy poet, struggling in a cottage, — what a contrast! And there is contrast also between him and the philosopher nestling in the English Church. Of the poet I say nothing, except that he was born 25th January, 1759, and died 21st July, 1796, in the thirty-seventh year of his age.

There is only a slender thread of Burns to be woven into this web, and yet, coming from him, it must not be neglected. In a letter dated 8th November, 1788, after a friendly word for the unfortunate house of Stuart, he prophetically alludes to American independence : —

" I will not, I cannot, enter into the merits of the cause, but I dare say the American Congress, in 1776, will be allowed to be as able and as enlightened as the English Convention was in 1688 ; *and that their posterity will celebrate the centenary of their deliverance from us, as duly and sincerely as we do ours from the oppressive measures of the house of Stuart."* [2]

---

[1] Meadley, Memoirs of Paley, p. 383. Appendix G.
[2] Currie, Life and Works of Burns, p. 266. Grahame, History of United States, Vol. IV. p. 462.

The year 1788, when these words were written, was a year of commemoration, being the hundredth from the famous revolution by which the Stuarts were excluded from the throne of England. The "centenary" of our independence is not yet completed; but long ago the commemoration began. On the coming of that hundredth anniversary, the prophecy of Burns will be more than fulfilled.

This aspiration is in harmony with the address to George III. in the "Dream," after the loss of the Colonies: —

> "Your royal nest, beneath your wing,
> Is e'en right reft and clouted "; —

meaning broken and patched; also with the obnoxious toast he gave at a supper, "May our success in the present war be equal to the justice of our cause";[1] and also with the "Ode on the American War,"[2] beginning, —

> "No Spartan tube, no Attic shell,
> No lyre Eolian, I awake;
> 'T is Liberty's bold note I swell;
> Thy harp, Columbia, let me take."

How natural for the great poet, who had pictured the sublime brotherhood of man : —

> "Then let us pray, that come it may,
> And come it will, for a' that,
> That man to man, the wide world o'er,
> Shall brothers be and a' that.[3]

---

[1] The MS. of a letter from Burns, mentioning the incident, is preserved by Stevens in his Bibliotheca Geographica, Part I. p. 58 (1872).

[2] Ibid., p. 57.

[3] Béranger reproduced the same life-giving cosmopolitan sentiment: —

> "Peuples, formez une sainte alliance,
> Et donnez-vous la main."

RICHARD BRINSLEY SHERIDAN, 1794.

SHERIDAN was a genius, who united the palm of eloquence in Parliament with that other palm won at the theatre. His speeches and his plays excited equal applause. The House of Commons and Drury Lane were the scenes of his famous labors, while society enjoyed his graceful wit. He was born in Dublin, September, 1751, and died in London, July 7th, 1816.

I quote now from a speech in the House of Commons, 21st January, 1794.

"America remains neutral, prosperous, and at peace! America, with a wisdom, prudence, and magnanimity which we have disdained, thrives at this moment in a state of envied tranquillity, and *is hourly clearing the paths of unbounded opulence.* America has monopolized the commerce and the advantages which we have abandoned. O, turn your eyes to her; view her situation, her happiness, her content; observe her trade and her manufactures adding daily to her general credit, to her private enjoyments, and to her public resources, *her name and government rising above the nations of Europe with a simple but commanding dignity, that wins at once the respect, the confidence, and the affection of the world.*" [1]

Here is true respect and sympathy for our country, with a forecast of increasing prosperity, and an image of her attitude among the nations. It is pleasant to enroll the admired author of "The Rivals" and "The School for Scandal" in this catalogue.

[1] Hansard, Parliamentary History, Vol. XXX. pp. 1219, 1220.

FOX, 1794.

In quoting from Charles James Fox, the statesman, minister, and orator, I need add nothing, except that he was born 24th January, 1749, and died 13th September, 1806, and that he was an early friend of our country.

Many words of his, especially during our Revolution, might be introduced here ; but I content myself with a single passage of later date, which, besides its expression of good-will, is a prophecy of our power. It is found in a speech on his motion for putting an end to war with France in the House of Commons, 30th May, 1794.

" It was impossible to dissemble that we had a serious dispute with America, and although we might be confident that the wisest and best man of his age, who presided in the government of that country, would do everything that became him to avert a war, it was impossible to foresee the issue. America had no fleet, no army ; but in case of war she would find various means to harass and annoy us. Against her we could not strike a blow that would not be as severely felt in London as in America, so identified were the two countries by commercial intercourse. *To a contest with such an adversary he looked as the greatest possible misfortune.* If we commenced another crusade against her, we might destroy her trade, and check the progress of her agriculture, but we must also equally injure ourselves. Desperate, therefore, indeed, must be that war in which each wound inflicted on our enemy would at the same time inflict one upon ourselves. He hoped to God that such an event as a war with America would not happen." [1]

All good men on both sides of the ocean must join with Fox, who thus early deprecated war between the

---

[1] Parliamentary History, Vol. XXXI. p. 627.

United States and England, and portrayed the fearful
consequences. Time, which has enlarged and multi-
plied the relations between the two countries, makes
his words more applicable now than when first uttered.

THE ABBÉ GRÉGOIRE, 1808.

HENRI GRÉGOIRE, of France, Curate, Deputy to the
States General, Constitutional Bishop, Member of the
Convention, also of the Council of Five Hundred, and
Senator, sometimes called Bishop, more frequently Abbé,
was born 4th December, 1750, and died 28th April, 1831.
To these titles add Abolitionist and Republican.

His character and career were unique, being in France
what Clarkson and Wilberforce were in England, and
much more, for he was not only an Abolitionist. In
all history no hero of humanity stands forth more conspicuous for instinctive sympathy with the Rights of
Man and constancy in their support. As early as 1788
he signalized himself by an essay, crowned by the
Academy of Metz, upholding tolerance for the Jews.[1]
His public life began while yet a curate, as a representative of the clergy of Lorraine in the States General,
but his sympathies with the people were at once manifest. In the engraving by which the oath in the tennis
court is commemorated he appears in the foreground.
His votes were always for the enfranchisement of the
people and the improvement of their condition, his
hope being "to Christianize the Revolution." In the
night session of 4th August, 1789, he declared for the
abolition of privileges. He was the first to give adhe-
sion to the civil constitution of the clergy, and himself

[1] Essai sur la Régénération physique et morale des Juifs.

became a constitutional bishop. The decree abolishing royalty was drawn by him, and he avows that for many days thereafter the excess of joy took from him appetite and sleep. In the discussion on the execution of the king he called for the suppression of the punishment of death. At his instance the convention abolished African slavery. With similar energy he sustained public libraries, botanical gardens, and experimental farms. He was a founder of the Bureau of Longitudes, the *Conservatoire des Arts et Métiers*, and of the National Institute. More than any person he contributed to prevent the destruction of public monuments, and was the first to call this crime " vandalism," — an excellent term, since adopted in all European languages. With similar vigor he said, in words often quoted, " Kings are in the moral order what monsters are in the physical order"; and, " The history of kings is the martyrology of the people." He denounced " the oligarchs of all countries and all the crowned brigands who pressed down the people," and, according to his own boast, " spat upon " duellists. " Better a loss to deplore than an injustice to reproach ourselves with," was his lofty solace as he turned from the warning that the Colonies might be endangered by the rights he demanded.

Such a man could not reconcile himself to the Empire or to Napoleon; nor could he expect consideration under the Restoration. But he was constant always to his original sentiments. In 1826 he wrote a work with the expressive title, " The Nobility of the Skin, or the Prejudice of Whites against the Color of Africans and that of their black and mixed Descendants." [1] His life

---

[1] De la noblesse de la peau ou du préjugé des blancs contre la couleur des Africains et celle de leurs descendants noir et sang-mêlé.

was prolonged to witness the Revolution of 1830, and shortly after his remains were borne to the cemetery of Mont Parnasse by young men, who took the horses from the hearse.[1]

This brief account of one little known is an introduction to signal prophecies concerning America.

As early as 8th June, 1791, in a document addressed to citizens of color and free negroes of the French islands,[2] he boldly said : —

"A day will come when deputies of color will traverse the ocean to come and sit in the national diet and to swear with us to live and die under our laws. A day will come when the sun will not shine among you except upon freemen, — when the rays of the light-spreading orb will no longer fall upon irons and slaves. . . . . It is according to the irresistible march of events and the progress of intelligence, that all people dispossessed of the domain of liberty will at last recover this indefeasible property." [3]

These strong and confident words, so early in date, were followed by others more remarkable. At the conclusion of his admirable work *De la Littérature des Nègres*, first published in 1808, where, with equal knowledge and feeling, homage is done to a people wronged and degraded by man, he cites his prediction with regard to the sun shining only upon freemen, and then, elevated by the vision, declares that "the American Continent, asylum of liberty, is moving towards an order of things which will be common to the Antilles, and *the course of which all the powers combined cannot*

7 *

arrest." [1]   This vigorous language is crowned by a prophecy of singular extent and precision, when, after dwelling on the influences at work to accelerate progress, he foretells the eminence of our country : —

"When an energetic and powerful nation, to which everything presages high destinies, stretching its arms upon the two oceans, Atlantic and Pacific, shall direct its vessels from one to the other *by an abridged route, — it may be in cutting the isthmus of Panama; it may be in forming a canal communicating, as has been proposed, by the river St. John and the lake of Nicaragua, — it will change the face of the commercial world and the face of empires.* Who knows if America will not then avenge the outrages she has received, and if our old Europe, placed in the rank of a subaltern power, will not become a colony of the New World?" [2]

Thus resting on the two oceans with a canal between, so that the early "secret of the strait" shall no longer exist, the American Republic will change the face of the world, and perhaps make Europe subaltern. Such was the vision of the French Abolitionist, lifted by devotion to Humanity.

THOMAS JEFFERSON, 1824.

SMALL preface is needed for the testimony of Jefferson, whose life belongs to the history of his country: He was born 2d April, 1743, and died 4th July, 1826.

Contemporary and rival of Adams, the author of the Declaration of Independence surpassed the other in sympathetic comprehension of the Rights of Man, as the other surpassed him in the prophetic spirit. Jefferson's words picturing slavery were unequalled in the

[1] Page 282.   [2] Page 283.

prolonged discussion of that terrible subject, and his
two Inaugural Addresses are masterpieces of political
truth. But with clearer eye Adams foresaw the future
grandeur of the Republic, and dwelt on its ravishing
light and glory. The vision of our country, coextensive
and coincident with the North American Continent, was
never beheld by Jefferson. While recognizing that our
principles of government, traversing the Rocky Moun-
tains, would smite upon the Pacific coast, his sight did
not embrace the distant communities there as parts of a
common country. This is apparent in a letter to John
Jacob Astor, 24th March, 1812, where, referring to the
commencement of a settlement by the latter on Colum-
bia River, and declaring the gratification with which he
looked forward to the time when its descendants should
have spread through the whole length of that coast, he
adds, "covering it with free and independent Americans, *unconnected with us but by the ties of blood and
interest*, and employing like us the rights of self-government."[1] In another letter to Mr. Astor, 9th November, 1813, he characterizes the settlement as "the germ
of a great, free, and *independent empire on that side of
our continent*,"[2] thus carefully announcing political dis-
sociation.

But Jefferson has not been alone in blindness to the
mighty capabilities of the Republic, inspired by his own
Declaration of Independence. Daniel Webster, in a
speech at Faneuil Hall, as late as 7th November, 1848,
pronounced that the Pacific coast could not be governed from Europe or from the Atlantic side of the
Continent; and he pressed the absurdity of anything
different: —

[1] Jefferson, Writings, Vol. VI. p. 55.   [2] Ibid., p. 248.

"And now let me ask if there be any sensible man in the whole United States, who will say for a moment, that, when fifty or a hundred thousand persons of this description [Americans mainly, but all Anglo-Saxons] shall find themselves on the shores of the Pacific Ocean, they will long consent to be under the rules of the American Congress or the British Parliament. They will raise the standard for themselves, and they ought to do it." [1]

Such a precise and strenuous protest from such a quarter mitigates the distrust of Jefferson. But after the acquisition of California the orator said, " I willingly admit that my apprehensions have not been realized." [2]

On the permanence of the National Union, and its influence throughout the world, Jefferson prophesied thus, in a letter to Lafayette, 14th February, 1815 : —

" The cement of this Union is in the heart-blood of every American. I do not believe there is on earth a government established on so immovable a basis. Let them in any State, even in Massachusetts itself, raise the standard of separation, and its citizens will rise in mass and do justice to themselves on their own incendiaries." [3]

Unhappily the Rebellion shows that he counted too much on the patriotism of the States against "their own incendiaries." In the same hopeful spirit, he wrote to Edward Livingston, the eminent jurist, 4th April, 1824 : —

" You have many years yet to come of vigorous activity, and I confidently trust they will be employed in cherishing

<hr/>

[1] Boston Daily Advertiser, 9th November, 1848. This speech is not found in the collected works of Mr. Webster.
[2] Speech at Pilgrim Festival, New York, 1850: Works, Vol. II. p. 526.
[3] Writings, Vol. VI. p. 426.

every measure which may foster our brotherly union and
perpetuate a constitution of government *destined to be the
primitive and precious model of what is to change the condition
of man over the globe.*" [1]

In these latter words he takes his place on the platform of John Adams, and sees the world changed by
our example. But again he is anxious about the Union.
In another letter to Livingston, 25th March, 1825, after
saying of the National Constitution, that "it is a compact of many independent powers, every single one of
which claims an equal right to understand it and to re-
quire its observance," he prophesies : —

" However strong the cord of compact may be, there is a
point of tension at which it will break." [2]

Thus, in venerable years, while watching with anxiety the fortunes of the Union, the patriarch did not fail
to see the new order of ages instituted by the American
Government.

GEORGE CANNING, 1826.

GEORGE CANNING was a successor of Fox, in the
House of Commons, as statesman, minister, and orator ;
he was born 11th April, 1770, and died 8th August,
1827, in the beautiful villa of the Duke of Devonshire,
at Chiswick, where Fox had died before. Unlike Fox
in sentiment for our country, he is nevertheless associated with a leading event of our history, and is the
author of prophetic words.

The Monroe Doctrine, as now familiarly called, proceeded from Canning. He was its inventor, promoter,

---

[1] Writings, Vol. VII. p. 344.   [2] Ibid., p. 404.

and champion, at least so far as it bears against European intervention in American affairs. Earnestly engaged in counteracting the designs of the Holy Alliance for the restoration of the Spanish colonies to Spain, he sought to enlist the United States in the same policy; and when Mr. Rush, our Minister at London, replied that any interference with European politics was contrary to the traditions of the American Government, he argued that, however just such a policy might have been formerly, it was no longer applicable, — that the question was new and complicated, — that it was "full as much American as European, to say no more," — that it concerned the United States under aspects and interests as immediate and commanding as those of any of the states of Europe, — that "they were the first power on that continent, and confessedly the leading power"; and he then asked, "Was it possible that they could see with indifference their fate decided upon by Europe? Had not a new epoch arrived in the relative position of the United States toward Europe, which Europe must acknowledge? *Were the great political and commercial interests*, which hung upon the destinies of the new continent to be canvassed and adjusted in this hemisphere, without the co-operation, or even the knowledge, of the United States?" With mingled ardor and importunity the British Minister pressed his case. At last, after much discussion in the Cabinet at Washington, President Monroe, accepting the lead of Mr. Canning and with the counsel of John Quincy Adams, put forth his famous declaration, where, after referring to the radical difference between the political systems of Europe and America, he says, that "we should consider any attempt on their part to extend their systems to any portion of this hemisphere as *dangerous to our peace and safety,*" and that, where governments have been recognized by us as independent, " we could not view any interposition for the purpose of oppressing them, or controlling in any other manner their destiny, by any European power, in any other light than as *a manifestation of an unfriendly disposition toward the United States.*" [1]

The message of President Monroe was received in England with enthusiastic congratulations. It was upon all tongues; the press was full of it; the securities of Spanish America rose in the market; the agents of Spanish America were happy.[2] Brougham exclaimed, in Parliament, that " no event had ever dispersed greater joy, exultation, and gratitude over all the freemen of Europe." Mackintosh rejoiced in the coincidence of England and the United States, " the two great commonwealths, for so he delighted to call them ; and he heartily prayed that they may be forever united in the cause of justice and liberty." [3] The Holy Alliance abandoned their purposes on this continent, and the independence of Spanish America was established. Some time afterwards, on the occasion of assistance to Portugal, when Mr. Canning felt called to review and vindicate his foreign policy, he assumed the following lofty strain. This was in the House of Commons, 12th December, 1826 : — *

" It would be disingenuous not to admit that the entry of the French army into Spain was, in a certain sense, a

[1] Annual Message to Congress of 2d December, 1823.

[2] Rush, Memoranda of Residence at London, Vol. II. p. 458; Wheaton, Elements of International Law, pp. 97 – 112, Dana's note.

[3] Stapleton, Life of Canning, Vol. II. pp. 46, 47.

disparagement, an affront to our pride, a blow to the feelings of England. But I deny that, questionable or censurable as the act may be, it was one that necessarily called for our direct and hostile opposition. Was nothing then to be done? If France occupied Spain, was it necessary, in order to avoid the consequences of that occupation, that we should blockade Cadiz? No. I looked another way. I sought materials for compensation in another hemisphere. Contemplating Spain, such as our ancestors had known her, I resolved that, if France had Spain, it should not be Spain 'with the Indies.' *I called the New World into existence to redress the balance of the Old.*" [1]

If the republics of Spanish America, thus summoned into independent existence, have not contributed the weight thus vaunted, the growing power of the United States is ample to compensate deficiencies on this continent. There is no balance of power it cannot redress.

ALEXIS DE TOCQUEVILLE, 1835.

With De Tocqueville we come among contemporaries removed by death. He was born at Paris, 29th July, 1805, and died at Cannes, 16th April, 1859. Having known him personally and seen him at his castle-home in Normandy, I cannot fail to recognize the man in his writings, which on this account have a double charm.

He was the younger son of noble parents, his father being of ancient Norman descent and his mother granddaughter of Malesherbes, the venerated defender of Louis XVI.; but his aristocratic birth had no influence to check the generous sympathies with which his heart always palpitated. In 1831 he came to America as a

---

[1] Canning, Speeches, Vol. VI. pp. 108, 109.

commissioner from the French Government to examine our prisons, but with a larger commission from his own soul to study republican institutions. His conscientious application, rare probity, penetrating thought, and refinement of style all appeared in his work, *De la Démocratie en Amérique*, first published in 1835, whose peculiar success is marked by the fourteenth French edition now before me, and the translations into other languages. At once he was famous and his work classical. The Academy opened its gates. Since Montesquieu there had been no equal success in the same department, and he was constantly likened to the illustrious author of "The Spirit of Laws." Less epigrammatic, less artful, and less French than his prototype, he was more simple, truthful, and prophetic. A second publication in 1840 with the same title, the fruit of mature studies, presented American institutions in another aspect, exhibiting his unimpaired faith in Democracy, which with him was Equality as "first principle and symbol."[1]

Entering the French Chambers, he became eminent for character, discussing chiefly those measures in which civilization is most concerned, — the reform of prisons, the abolition of slavery, penal colonies, and the pretensions of socialism. His work, *L'Ancien Régime et la Révolution*, awakens admiration, while his correspondence is among the most charming in literature, exciting love as well as delight.

His honest and practical insight made him philosopher and prophet, which he was always. A speech in the Chambers, 27th January, 1848, was memorable as predicting the Revolution which occurred two months

[1] Vol. III. Chap. VII. p. 527.

later. But his foresight with regard to America brings him into our procession.

His clearness of vision appears in the distinctness with which he recognized the peril from slavery and from the pretensions of the States. And in slavery he saw also the prolonged and diversified indignity to the African race. This was his statement:—

"The most fearful of all the evils which menace the future of the United States springs from *the presence of the blacks on their soil.* When we seek the cause of present embarrassments and of future dangers to the United States, we arrive almost always at this first fact, from whatever point we depart."[1]

Then with consummate power he depicts the lot of the unhappy African even when free,— oppressed, but with whites for judges; shut out from the jury; his son excluded from the school which receives the descendant of the European; unable with gold to buy a place at the theatre "by the side of him who was his master"; in hospitals separated from the rest; permitted to worship the same God as the whites, but not to pray at the same altar; and when life is passed the difference of condition prevailing still even over the equality of the grave.[2]

Impressed by the menace from slavery, he further pictures the Union succumbing to the States:—

"I deceive myself, or the Federal Government of the United States tends daily to weaken itself. It withdraws successively from affairs; it restricts more and more the circle of its action. Naturally feeble, it abandons even the appearance of force."[3]

[1] De la Démocratie en Amérique, Tom. II. Chap. X. p. 302 (ed. 1864).
[2] Ibid., p. 307.
[3] Ibid., Tom. II. Chap. X. p. 397.

Such was the condition when De Tocqueville wrote,
and so it continued until the Rebellion broke forth and
the country rose to save the Union. Foreseeing this
peril, he did not despair of the Republic, which, in his
judgment, was "the natural state of the Americans," [1]
with roots more profound than the Union.

In describing the future he becomes a prophet. Accepting the conclusion that the number of inhabitants
doubles in twenty-two years, and not recognizing any
causes to arrest this progressive movement, he foresees
the colossal empire: —

"The Americans of the United States, whatever they do,
will become one of the greatest people of the earth; they
will cover with their offshoots almost all North America.
The continent which they inhabit is their domain; it cannot escape them." [2]

Then, declaring that the "English race," not stopping
within the limits of the Union, will advance much beyond towards the northeast, — that at the northwest
they will encounter only Russian settlements without
importance, that at the southwest the vast solitudes
of Mexican territory will be appropriated, — and dwelling on the fortunate geographical position of "the English of America," with their climate, their interior seas,
their great rivers, and the fertility of their soil, he is
ready to say: —

"So in the midst of the uncertainty of the future there
is at least one event which is certain. At an epoch which
we can call near, since it concerns the life of a people,
the Anglo-Americans alone will cover all the immense territory comprised between the polar ice and the tropics; they

[1] De la Démocratie en Amérique, Tom. II. Chap. X. p. 399 (ed. 1864).
[2] Ibid., p. 379.

will spread from the shores of the Atlantic Ocean even to the coasts of the Southern Sea." [1]

Then, declaring that the territory destined to the Anglo-American race equals three fourths of Europe, that many centuries will pass before the different offshoots of this race will cease to present a common physiognomy, that no epoch can be foreseen when in the New World there will be any permanent inequality of conditions, and that there are processes of association and of knowledge by which the people are assimilated with each other and with the rest of the world, the prophet speaks : —

"There will then arrive a time when there will be seen in North America one hundred and fifty millions of men, equal together, who will all belong to the same family, who will have the same point of departure, the same civilization, the same language, the same religion, the same habits, the same manners, and over which thought will circulate in the same form and paint itself in the same colors. All else is doubtful, but this is certain. Here is a fact entirely new in the world, of which imagination can hardly seize the extent." [2]

No American can fail to be strengthened in the future of the Republic by the testimony of De Tocqueville. Honor and gratitude to his memory !

RICHARD COBDEN, 1849.

COMING yet nearer to our own day, we meet a familiar name, now consecrated by death,— Richard Cobden ; born 3d June, 1804, and died 2d April, 1865. In

[1] De la Démocratie en Amérique Tom. II. Chap. X. p. 428 (ed. 1864).
[2] Ibid., p. 430.

proportion as truth prevails among men, his character will shine with increasing glory until he is recognized as the first Englishman of his time. Though thoroughly English, he was not insular. He served mankind as well as England.

His masterly faculties and his real goodness made him a prophet always. He saw the future, and strove to hasten its promises. The elevation and happiness of the human family were his daily thought. He knew how to build as well as to destroy. Through him disabilities upon trade and oppressive taxes were overturned; also a new treaty was negotiated with France, quickening commerce and intercourse. He was never so truly eminent as when bringing his practical sense and enlarged experience to commend the cause of Permanent Peace in the world by the establishment of a refined system of International Justice, and the disarming of the nations. To this great consummation all his later labors tended. I have before me a long letter, dated at London, 7th November, 1849, where he says much on this absorbing question, from which, by an easy transition, he passes to speak of the proposed annexation of Canada to the United States. As what he says on the latter topic concerns America, and is a prophetic voice, I have obtained permission to copy it for this collection: —

"Race, religion, language, traditions, are becoming bonds of union, and not the parchment title-deeds of sovereigns. These instincts may be thwarted for the day, but they are too deeply rooted in nature and in usefulness not to prevail in the end. I look with less interest to these struggles of races to live apart for what they want to undo, than for what they will prevent being done in future. *They will warn rulers that henceforth the acquisition of fresh territory, by force of arms, will only bring embarrassments and civil war,* instead of that increased strength which, in ancient times, when people were passed, like flocks of sheep, from one king to another, always accompanied the incorporation of new territorial conquests.

"This is the secret of the admitted doctrine, that we shall have no more wars of conquest or ambition. In this respect *you* are differently situated, having vast tracts of unpeopled territory to tempt that cupidity which, in respect of landed property, always disposes individuals and nations, however rich in acres, to desire more. This brings me to the subject of Canada, to which you refer in your letters.

"I agree with you, that *nature has decided that Canada and the United States must become one, for all purposes of free intercommunication.* Whether they also shall be united in the same federal government must depend upon the two parties to the union. I can assure you that there will be no repetition of the policy of 1776, on our part, to prevent our North American colonies from pursuing their interest in their own way. If the people of Canada are tolerably unanimous in wishing to sever the very slight thread which now binds them to this country. I see no reason why, if good faith and ordinary temper be observed, it should not be done amicably. I think it would be far more likely to be accomplished peaceably *if the subject of annexation were left as a distinct question.* I am quite sure that *we* should be gainers, to the amount of about a million sterling annually, if our North American colonists would set up in life for themselves and maintain their own establishments, and I see no reason to doubt that they might be also gainers by being thrown upon their own resources.

"The less your countrymen mingle in the controversy, the better. It will only be an additional obstacle in the path of those in this country who see the ultimate necessity of a separation, but who have still some ignorance and prejudice to contend against, which, if used as political capital by designing politicians, may complicate seriously a very difficult piece of statesmanship. It is for you and such as you, who love peace, to guide your countrymen aright in this matter. You have made the most noble contributions of any modern writer to the cause of peace; and as a public man I hope you will exert all your influence to induce Americans to hold a dignified attitude and observe a 'masterly inactivity' in the controversy which is rapidly advancing to a solution between the mother country and her American colonies."

A prudent patriotism among us will appreciate the wisdom of this counsel, more needed now than when written. The controversy which Cobden foresaw "between the mother country and her American colonies" is yet undetermined. The recent creation of what is somewhat grandly called "The Dominion of Canada" marks one stage in its progress.

LUCAS ALAMAN, 1852.

FROM Canada I pass to Mexico, and close this list with Lucas Alaman, the Mexican statesman and historian, who has left on record a most pathetic prophecy with regard to his own country, intensely interesting to us at this moment.

Alaman was born in the latter part of the last century, and died June 2, 1853. He was a prominent leader of the monarchical party, and Minister of Foreign Affairs under Presidents Bustamente and Santa Ana. In this capacity he inspired the respect of foreign diplomatists. One of these, who had occasion to know him officially, says of him, in answer to my inquiries, that he "was the greatest statesman Mexico has produced since her independence."[1]   He was one of the few in any country who have been able to unite literature with public life, and obtain honors in each.

His first work was "Dissertations on the History of the Mexican Republic,"[2] in three volumes, published at Mexico, 1844. In these he considers the original conquest by Cortes, its consequences, the conqueror and his family, the propagation of the Christian religion in New Spain, the formation of the city of Mexico, the history of Spain and the house of Bourbon. All these topics are treated somewhat copiously. Then followed the "History of Mexico, from the First Movements which prepared its Independence in 1808, to the present Epoch,"[3] in five volumes, published at Mexico, the first bearing date 1849, and the fifth 1852. From the Preface to the first volume, it appears that the author was born in Guanajuato, and witnessed there the beginning of the Mexican revolution in 1810, under Don Miguel Hidalgo, the curate of Dolores; that he was personally acquainted with the curate and with many who had a principal part in the successes of that time; that he was experienced in public affairs, as deputy and as member of the cabinet; and that he had known directly the persons and things of which he wrote. His last volume embraces the government of Iturbide as Emperor, and also his unfortunate death, ending with the establishment of the Mexican Federal

---

[1] The excellent Baron von Gerolt, for so long a period at Washington as Minister of Prussia and of the German Empire.

[2] Disertaciones sobre la Historia de la Republica Megicana.

[3] Historia de Mejico desde los primeros Movimientos que prepararon á su Independencia en al Año de 1808 hasta la Epoca presente.

Republic in 1824. The work is careful and well considered. The eminent diplomatist already mentioned, who had known the author officially, writes that "no one was better acquainted with the history and causes of the incessant revolutions in his unfortunate country, and that his work on this subject is considered by all respectable men in Mexico a *chef-d'œuvre* for purity of sentiments and patriotic convictions."

It is on account of the valedictory words of this History that I introduce the name of Alaman, and nothing more striking appears in this gallery. Behold: —

"Mexico will be, without doubt, a land of prosperity from its natural advantages, *but it will not be so for the races which now inhabit it.* As it seemed the destiny of the peoples who established themselves therein at different and remote epochs to perish from the face of it, leaving hardly a memory of their existence; even as the nation which built the edifices of Palenque, and those which we admire in the peninsula of Yucatan, was destroyed without its being known what it was nor how it disappeared; *even as the Toltecs perished by the hands of barbarous tribes coming from the North,* no record of them remaining but the pyramids of Cholula and Teotihuacan; and, finally, even as the ancient Mexicans fell beneath the power of the Spaniards, *the country gaining infinitely by this change of dominion, but its ancient masters being overthrown;* — so likewise its present inhabitants shall be ruined and hardly obtain the compassion they have merited, and the Mexican nation of our days shall have applied to it what a celebrated Latin poet said of one of the most famous personages of Roman history, STAT MAGNI NOMINIS UMBRA,[1] — nothing more remains than the shadow of a name illustrious in another time.

[1] In the original text of Alaman this is printed in large capitals, and explained in a note as said by Lucan of Pompey.

8

"May the Almighty, in whose hands is the fate of nations, and who by ways hidden from our sight abases or exalts them, according to the designs of his providence, be pleased to grant unto ours the protection by which he has so often deigned to preserve it from the dangers to which it has been exposed."[1]

Most affecting words of prophecy! Considering the character of the author as statesman and historian, it could have been only with inconceivable anguish that he made this terrible record for the land whose child and servant he was. Born and reared in Mexico, honored by its important trusts, and writing the history of its independence, it was his country, having for him all that makes country dear; and yet thus calmly he consigns the present people to oblivion, while another enters into those happy places where nature is so bountiful. And so a Mexican leaves the door open to the foreigner.

CONCLUSION.

SUCH are prophetic voices, differing in character and importance, but all having one augury, and opening one vista, illimitable in extent and vastness. Farewell to the narrow thought of Montesquieu, that a republic can exist only in a small territory. Through representation and federation a continent is not too much for practical dominion, nor is it beyond expectation. Well did Webster say, "The prophecies and the poets are with us." And then again, "With regard to this country there is no poetry like the poetry of events, and all the prophecies lag behind the fulfilment."[2] But my purpose is not

[1] Historia, Tom. V. pp. 954, 955.
[2] Speech at the Festival of the Sons of New Hampshire, 7th November, 1849: Works, Vol. II. pp. 510, 511.

with the fulfilment, except as it stands forth visible to all.

Ancient prophecy foretold another world beyond the ocean, which in the mind of Christopher Columbus was nothing less than the Orient with its inexhaustible treasures. The continent was hardly known when the prophets began, — poets like Chapman, Drayton, Daniel, Herbert, Cowley, — economists like Child and Drayton, — New-Englanders like Morrill, Ward, and Sewall, — and, mingling with these, that rare genius, Sir Thomas Browne, who, in the reign of Charles II., while the settlements were in infancy, predicted their growth in power and civilization; and then that rarest character, Bishop Berkeley, who, in the reign of George I., while the settlements were still feeble and undeveloped, heralded a Western empire as "Time's noblest offspring."

These voices are general. Others more precise followed. Turgot, the philosopher and minister, saw in youth, with the vision of genius, that all colonies must at their maturity drop from the parent stem, like ripe fruit. John Adams, one of the chiefs of our own history, in a youth illumined as that of Turgot, saw the predominance of the Colonies in population and power, followed by the transfer of empire to America; then the glory of Independence and its joyous celebration by grateful generations; then the triumph of our language; and, finally, the establishment of our republican institutions over all North America. Then came the Abbé Galiani, the Neapolitan Frenchman, who, writing from Naples while our struggle was still undecided, gayly predicts the total downfall of Europe, the transmigration to America, and the consummation of the greatest revolution of the globe by establishing the reign of America over Europe. There is also Adam Smith, the illustrious philosopher, who quietly carries the seat of government across the Atlantic. Meanwhile Pownall, once a colonial governor and then a member of Parliament, in successive works of great detail, foreshadows independence, naval supremacy, commercial prosperity, immigration from the Old World, and a new national life, destined to supersede the systems of Europe and arouse the "curses" of royal ministers. Hartley, also a member of Parliament, and the British negotiator who signed the definitive treaty of Independence, bravely announces in Parliament that the New World is before the Colonists, and that liberty is theirs; and afterwards, as diplomatist, instructs his government that, through the attraction of our public lands, immigration will be quickened beyond precedent, and the national debt cease to be a burden. Aranda, the Spanish statesman and diplomatist, predicts to his king that the United States, though born a "pygmy," will soon be a "colossus," under whose influence Spain will lose all her American possessions except only Cuba and Porto Rico. Paley, the philosopher, hails our successful revolution as destined to accelerate the fall of slavery, which he denounces as an abominable tyranny. Burns, the truthful poet, who loved mankind, looks forward a hundred years, and beholds our people rejoicing in the centenary of their independence. Sheridan pictures our increasing prosperity, and the national dignity winning the respect, confidence, and affection of the world. Fox, the liberal statesman, foresees the increasing might and various relations of the United States, so that a blow aimed at them must have a rebound as destructive as itself. The Abbé Grégoire, devoted to the slave, whose freedom he predicts, describes the power and glory of the American Republic, resting on the two great oceans, and swaying the world. Tardily, Jefferson appears with anxiety for the National Union, and yet announcing our government as the familiar and precious model to change the condition of mankind. Canning, the brilliant orator, in a much-admired flight of eloquence, discerns the New World, with its republics just called into being, redressing the balance of the Old. De Tocqueville, while clearly foreseeing the peril from slavery, proclaims the future grandeur of the Republic, covering "almost all North America," and making the continent its domain, with a population, equal in rights, counted by the hundred million. Cobden, whose fame will be second only to that of Adam Smith among all in this catalogue, calmly predicts the separation of Canada from the mother country by peaceable means. Alaman, the Mexican statesman and historian, announces that Mexico, which has already known so many successive races, will hereafter be ruled by yet another people, taking the place of the present possessors ; and with these prophetic words, the patriot draws a pall over his country.

All these various voices, of different times and lands, mingle and intertwine in representing the great future of our Republic, which from small beginnings has already become great. It was at first only a grain of mustard-seed, " which is, indeed, the least of all seeds ; but when it is grown, it is the greatest among herbs, and becomes a tree, so that the birds of the air come and lodge in the branches thereof." Better still, it was only a little leaven, but it is fast leavening the whole continent. Nearly all who have prophesied speak of "America" or "North America," and not of any limited circle, colony, or state. It was so, at the beginning, with Sir Thomas Browne, and especially with Berkeley. During our Revolution the Colonies, struggling for independence, were always described by. this continental designation. They were already "America," or "North America," (and such was the language of Washington,) thus incidentally foreshadowing that coming time when the whole continent, with all its various states, shall be a Plural Unit, with one Constitution, one Liberty, and one Destiny. The theme was also taken up by the poet, and popularized in the often-quoted lines : —

> " No pent-up Utica contracts your powers,
> But the whole boundless continent is yours."[1]

Such grandeur may justly excite anxiety rather than pride, for duties are in corresponding proportion. There is occasion for humility also, as the individual considers his own insignificance in the transcendent mass. The tiny polyp, in unconscious life, builds the everlasting coral ; each citizen is little more than the industrious insect. The result is reached by the continuity of combined exertion. Millions of citizens, working in obedience to nature, can accomplish anything.

Of course, war is an instrumentality which true civilization disowns. Here some of our prophets have erred. Sir Thomas Browne was so much overshadowed by his own age, that his vision was darkened by "great armies," and even "hostile and piratical attacks" on

---

1 By Jonathan M. Sewall, in an epilogue to Addison's Tragedy of " Cato," written in 1778 for the Bow Street Theatre, Portsmouth, N. H.

Europe. It was natural that Aranda, schooled in worldly life, should imagine the new-born power ready to seize the Spanish possessions. Among our own countrymen, Jefferson looked to war for the extension of dominion. The Floridas, he says on one occasion, "are ours on the first moment of war, and until a war they are of no particular necessity to us."[1] Happily they were acquired in another way. Then again, while declaring that no constitution was ever before so calculated as ours for extensive empire and self-government, and insisting upon Canada as a component part, he calmly says that "this would be, of course, in the first war."[2] Afterwards, while confessing a longing for Cuba, "as the most interesting addition that could ever be made to our system of States," he says that "he is sensible this can never be obtained, even with her own consent, without war."[3] Thus at each stage is the baptism of blood. In much better mood the poet Bishop recognized empire as moving gently in the pathway of light. All this is much clearer now than when he prophesied.

It is easy to see that empire obtained by force is unrepublican, and offensive to the first principle of our Union, according to which all just government stands only on the consent of the governed. Our country needs no such ally as war. Its destiny is mightier than war. Through peace it will have everything. This is our talisman. Give us peace, and population will increase beyond all experience; resources of all kinds will multiply infinitely; arts will embellish the land

---

[1] Complete Works, Vol. V. p. 444.
[2] Ibid.
[3] Ibid., Vol. VII. p. 316. See also pp. 288, 299.

with immortal beauty; the name of Republic will be exalted, until every neighbor, yielding to irresistible attraction, seeks new life in becoming part of the great whole; and the national example will be more puissant than army or navy for the conquest of the world.

THE END.

Cambridge : Electrotyped and Printed by Welch, Bigelow, & Co.

"*Not ordinary addresses, — they remind us rather of the Orations of Demosthenes, — of times when men of note, endowed with the highest understanding, gave full vent to the feelings that possessed them, and stirred their country with a fervid eloquence which was all the more impressive because it related to the political circumstances in which their country was placed.*" —
EDINBURGH JOURNAL.

THE COMPLETE WORKS

OF

CHARLES SUMNER,

In Twelve elegant Crown 8vo Volumes, with Portrait,
Notes, and Index.

Price per volume, Fine English Cloth $3.00
"   "   "   Half Calf, Gilt Extra, Library Edition   5.00

PUBLISHED BY

LEE AND SHEPARD,

Nos. 41-45 Franklin Street, Boston.

ANNOUNCEMENT.

Messrs. LEE & SHEPARD respectfully announce the continuation and early completion of

THE WORKS OF CHARLES SUMNER.

The original prospectus was issued when the distinguished orator and statesman was in the midst of his honorable career, and had apparently before him all the evening of his life, for the revision of his ORATIONS, SPEECHES, and ADDRESSES. Notwithstanding his impaired health, he had labored with assiduity to arrange and perfect them; and before his death NINE VOLUMES had been published, and the tenth was given to the printers. Materials for two or more volumes, carefully prepared by himself, are now in the hands of friends who are fully acquainted with his opinions, and familiar with his intellectual methods.

From the time of his election, in 1851, to the U. S. Senate, Charles Sumner was constantly before the public as the leader and representative of the party of freedom; and the volumes of his speeches form of themselves a history of the United States for over twenty years. It is seldom that the lifetime of one man, still less the period of his public services, includes the beginning and end of a controversy, so momentous in character, so far-reaching in effect, as that which has lately resulted in establishing the doctrine that "FREEDOM IS NATIONAL."

The founders of the republic are deservedly honored; but the great leaders in the party of equal rights, whose labors have given us a country worth living for, and worth dying to defend, must claim equal honor and gratitude from the present generation and from posterity.

The value of Mr. Sumner's works to students of political history, to scholars, and all lovers of literature, cannot well be over-estimated. They will be welcomed as a fitting memorial of the long and brilliant services of the man whose name and fame are a part of the renown of his country.

This edition, of which nine volumes are now ready for delivery to subscribers, will be elegantly printed on tinted and plated paper, from new type, will contain an accurate portrait of Mr. Sumner, and will be furnished with a complete analytical and topical index.

SOLD ONLY BY SUBSCRIPTION.

LEE AND SHEPARD, Publishers,
Nos. 41-45 Franklin Street.

BUTLER AND FLEETWOOD, General Agents,
No. 47 Franklin Street, Boston.

Agents of experience and capacity wanted throughout the United States.

IN PREPARATION.

THE ONLY AUTHORIZED

LIFE OF CHARLES SUMNER,

From materials left in the hands of his literary executors by the distinguished Senator. It will be issued at an early day, and will be uniform with the Complete Works now in course of preparation.

The Publishers invite attention to the following extracts taken from the mass of communications and testimonials received from prominent and leading men on both sides of the Atlantic : —

From Francis Lieber.

The complete works of Senator Sumner will have a high value for the earnest student who desires to trace the causes of some of the greatest movements in our times, — the times of political Reformation. They will have a great value in point of Political Ethics, of Statesmanship (or what the ancients called Politics), and in point of the Psychology of our own nation, in point of the Law of Nations and for every English scholar and admirer of eloquence. Not only will the works of Senator Sumner, after whose title, in Rome, the words "Four Times in Succession" would have been put, be gladly received by every reflecting public man in America, but also by every high-minded Nationalist and lover of freedom in Europe.

From William Cullen Bryant.

I am glad to learn that Mr. Sumner's works are to be collected and published under his own superintendence and revision. He ranks among our most eminent public men, and never treats of any subject without shedding new light upon it, and giving us reason to admire both his ability and the extent and accuracy of his information.

From Ralph Waldo Emerson.

I learn with interest that you are preparing to publish a complete collection of Mr. Sumner's writings and speeches. They will be the history of the Republic in the last twenty-five years, as told by a brave, perfectly honest, and well-instructed man, with large social culture, and relations to all eminent persons. Few public men have left records more important, — none more blameless. Mr. Sumner's large ability, his careful education, his industry, his early dedication to public affairs, his power of exhaustive statement, and his pure character, — qualities rarely combined in one man, — have been the strength and pride of the Republic. In Massachusetts, the patriotism of his constituents has treated him with exceptional regard. The ordinary complaisances expected of a candidate have not been required of him, it being known that his service was one of incessant labor, and that he had small leisure to plead his own cause, and less to nurse his private interests. There will be the more need of the careful publication in a permanent form of these vindications of political liberty and morality.

I hope that Mr. Sumner's contributions to some literary journals will not be omitted in your collection.

From John G. Whittier.

It gives me much satisfaction to learn that the entire speeches of Mr. Sumner are about to be published. Apart from their great merit in a literary and scholastic point of view, and as exhaustive arguments upon questions of the highest import, they have a certain historic value which will increase with the lapse of time. Whoever wishes to understand the legislation and political and moral progress of the country for the last quarter of a century, must study these remarkable speeches. I am heartily glad the publication has been determined upon, and wish it the success it deserves.

From Horace Greeley.

I hail it as a cheering sign of the times that the speeches and writings of Charles Sumner are to be published complete. We live in an age of inconsiderate gabble, when too many make speeches " on the spur of the moment," and " now that I am up," say whatever may chance to come into their heads. Mr. Sumner sufficiently respects his associates and his countrymen to speak with due preparation, and only when he feels that silence would be dereliction. " Not to stir without great arguments " is his rule; hence his speeches are not only a part of his country's history, but a very creditable and instructive part of it. In an age of venality and of reckless calumny, no man has ever doubted the purity of his motives, the singleness of his aims; and if the august title of statesman has been deserved by any American of his age, he is that American. I trust his collected writings will receive wide currency, as I am sure they will command universal consideration.

From Samuel G. Howe.

I think that your proposed edition of Mr. Sumner's Speeches will do much good. His public career teaches a lesson which should be learned by all who aspire to usefulness and true greatness. The source of his popularity and influence, creditable alike to him and to the people, is an intuitive perception of the right and firm faith in its prevalence. To him, whatever is right is ever expedient. Be the political horizon ever so dark, he knows the direction of the pole-star, and steers boldly towards it. In opposing storms, while ordinary politicians, like sailing ships, tack and keep as near the wind as seems safe, he, like the steamer, steers straight in the wind's eye; and though he may, for the moment, make no headway, he swerves not, larboard nor starboard. Most statesmen and politicians represent certain doctrines or party interests; while he represents the moral sense of the people. Where that sense is most developed, there he is best understood and most esteemed. A new edition of his Speeches will help to develop it still more; and it is for that end, rather than building a monument to him, that his friends ought to co-operate for your success.

From Caleb Cushing.

I think the speeches, discourses, and miscellaneous papers of Mr. Sumner eminently deserve to be collected and published in a complete form. Whatever difference of opinion there may be in the country concerning the various political doctrines which in his long Senatorial career he has so earnestly and so steadily maintained, certain it is that his productions constitute an essential part of our public history as well in foreign as in domestic relations; and they are characterized by such qualities of superior intellectual power, cultivated eloquence, and great and general accomplishment and statesmanship, as entitle them to a high and permanent place in the political literature of the United States.

From *James Russell Lowell.*

I am glad to hear that you have undertaken an edition of Mr. Sumner's collected works. There is a manifest propriety in this, for not only has he made many contributions to literature proper, but his speeches have been elaborated with so much care, and illustrated from so wide a field of reading, that letters claim in them an equal share with politics. Whatever view may be taken of them, they form an essential part of our history for the last twenty years.

Though I have sometimes been unable to go along with Mr. Sumner in his application of opinions, with which I mainly agreed, to questions of immediate policy, I have always duly honored the sincerity of his convictions, and his courage in maintaining them. A life of high aims, public purposes, and sustained integrity, has been fully rewarded by a constituency of which that which he represents in the Senate forms but a small portion, and I cannot doubt that your enterprise will be welcomed as it deserves by all who know how to appreciate an eloquence which has so largely confined itself to the discussion of principles, and a culture which is an ornament to the Senate.

From *George William Curtis.*

I am very glad to learn that the complete works of Charles Sumner will soon be published.

Mr. Sumner's public life has been illustrious for his unswerving devotion to human liberty, and his service in the great struggle of the last twenty years will be always gratefully remembered. Even the qualities that now alienate a certain sympathy will then be seen to have been necessary to his work.

His speeches are an essential part of the history of those times, and are distinguished by their ample knowledge and their lofty tone. There is no American citizen who may not study his works with instruction, no American statesman who may not contemplate his career with advantage.

From Benjamin F. Butler.

I am much pleased to learn that a complete compilation of Mr. Sumner's speeches and letters is to be published.

They are a desideratum for the times. The history of the anti-slavery contest in Congress is therein written in living language, because each speech made of itself an epoch in the struggle. The almost providential accident of one vote gave to Mr. Sumner the position of leader in the great work which has purged the institutions, the very constitution of the country, from the sin and wrong of slavery; and nobly has he filled it; better, indeed, than could have been done by any other man in the nation. The virulent opposition which he met in the great task which he undertook required his varied accomplishments and learning, his untiring industry, and unswerving devotion to principle, — qualities seldom united in one. The history of the regeneration of Republican Democracy in the western world would not be complete without the volumes you are about to publish.

From Henry Wilson.

I am really gratified to learn that you are to publish the complete works of Mr. Sumner, under his own supervision. During the past twenty-five years I have known him, watched his course as a public man, heard and read his speeches, and know how he has consecrated talents and learning to the rights of man and the enduring interests of his country. His speeches have largely contributed to produce the grand results that cheer and bless us, and I am sure they will be read with increasing interest, not only for the topics discussed, but for their learning and eloquence.

From Wendell Phillips.

I am glad you are to give us a complete collection of Mr. Sumner's Speeches. His part and place have been such in the last twenty years, that his career is largely the history of the Nation. His speeches cover the most important and interesting questions we have been called to meet. Years ago the easy sneer was that he was a man of "one idea," — dealt only with one question, or one class of questions.

But Mr. Sumner has been one of the most industrious, perhaps the most industrious, Senator that Massachusetts has ever given to the national councils. His mind has been more comprehensive than that of any of his predecessors. He has grappled with all the great problems of the day ; and so thoroughly, so exhaustively, as to leave nothing to desire.

Accurate, profoundly learned, always in the van, fearless, wielding a most commanding influence, his speeches will be the most valuable contribution possible to the literature of politics and reform. They have "made history," and will naturally be the best reliance of those who shall study our times, as his career will be, both for students and statesmen, one of the noblest examples.

By Hon. John P. Hale, in the United States Senate, August 27, 1851, in the debate after Mr. Sumner's Speech entitled " Freedom National, Slavery Sectional."

I feel bound to say that the Honorable Senator from Massachusetts has, so far as his own personal fame and reputation are concerned, done enough, by the effort he has made here to-day to place himself side by side with the first orators of antiquity, and as far ahead of any living American orator as freedom is ahead of slavery. I believe he has founded a new era to-day in the history of the politics and of the eloquence of the country; and that, in future generations, the young men of this nation will be stimulated to effort by the record of what an American Senator has this day done, to which all the appeals drawn from ancient history would be entirely inadequate. Yes, sir, he has to-day made a draft upon the gratitude of the friends of humanity and of liberty that will not be paid through many generations, and the memory of which shall endure as long as the English language is spoken, or the history of this Republic forms part of the annals of the world. That, sir, is what I feel, and if I had one other feeling, or could indulge in it in reference to that effort, it would be a feeling alway, that it was not in me to tread, even at a humble distance, in the path he has so nobly and eloquently illustrated.

From Hannibal Hamlin.

I learn with great pleasure that the complete works of Hon. Charles Sumner are being now prepared, and will soon be published.

The high position which Mr. Sumner has so long and so honorably maintained as one of the leading minds of the nation, his intimate connection with and lead in the great measure of the abolition of slavery, and all the great questions of the late war, and those involved in a just settlement of the same, render it a desideratum that his works should be published.

From S. Austin Allibone.

I have been in the habit for some years past, from time to time, of urging my valued friend, Mr. Sumner, to publish a collective edition of his speeches. You may therefore imagine the pleasure with which I have received the announcement that you are now engaged in the publication of a uniform edition of his complete works.

One of the favorite pupils of Judge Story, who considered him rather as a son than as his pupil (see Story's Life and Letters, Vol. II. p. 39), the endeared friend of Prescott, Wheaton, the Earl of Carlisle, and many of the most distinguished scholars on both sides of the Atlantic, Mr. Sumner's opportunities of instruction by contact with great minds have matured the scholarship of which the broad and deep foundations were laid in the laborious days and nights of collegiate and private application.

The " fulness " of his mind and the ease with which he draws from the vast stores of memory " things new and old " to illustrate the truths which he enforces, the errors he exposes, or the themes he propounds, are indeed marvellous ! See for instance, his oration, entitled, " The Scholar, the Jurist, the Artist, the Philanthropist," (1846), of which Prescott wrote : " I have read or rather listened to it, notes and all, with the greatest interest ; and when I say that my expectations have not been disappointed after having heard it cracked up so, I think you will think it praise enough. The most happy conception has been carried out admirably, as if it were the most natural order of things, without the least constraint or violence." (Ticknor's Life of Prescott, p. 378.) Among his late speeches, take his graphic and glowing portraiture of Alaska, over the sterile soil of which the light of his genius has cast a glow of bloom and beauty; which as a geographical and topographical monograph might have excited the envy of D'Anville or Humboldt. A complete collection of his works, fully rounded by a copious analytical index of subjects discussed, topics referred to, and facts adduced, would be an invaluable treasury to the scholar, the historian, and the general reader.

From Edwin P. Whipple.

I am glad to hear that a complete edition of Senator Sumner's works is to be published.

Not to speak of the eminent literary merit of his speeches and addresses, they are specially valuable as having contributed in an important degree to "make history" during the past twenty-five years. Many of his senatorial efforts are not so much speeches as events. They have palpably advanced the cause of honesty, justice, freedom, and humanity. It is to the immense honor of Massachusetts that she has had for so long a time so noble a representative in Washington of her sentiments and ideas, — one whose abundant learning, richness and reach of thought, and statesman-like forethought are combined with a philanthropy so frank and a spirit so intrepid.

A complete edition of the works of a statesman so variously endowed, and who has treated so many subjects with such a masterly command of knowledge, reasoning, and eloquence, cannot fail to be widely circulated.

From Hunt's Merchants' Magazine.

The Orations of Mr. Sumner belong to the literature of America. They are as far superior to the endless number of orations and speeches which are delivered throughout the country as the works of a polished, talented, and accomplished author surpass the ephemeral productions of a day. Pure and highly classical in style, strong in argument, and rich and glowing in imagery, and in some parts almost reaching the poetic, they come to the reader always fresh, always interesting and attractive. In one respect these orations surpass almost all others. It is in the elevation of sentiment, the high and lofty moral tone and grandeur of thought which they possess. In this particular, united with their literary merit, these productions have no equal among us. The one on the "True Grandeur of Nations" stands forth by itself, like a serene and majestic image, cut from the purest Parian marble. Those on "Peace and War," and two or three others, possess equal merit, equal beauty, and equal purity and dignity of thought. In our view, these orations approach nearer the models of antiquity than those of any other writer amongst us, unless it be Webster, whom Sumner greatly surpasses in moral tone and dignity of thought.

Many of the distinguished statesmen and scholars of our country, now deceased, left on record their opinion of the character and value of Mr. Sumner's public services. From among these a few are selected.

From John Quincy Adams.

In a letter addressed to Mr. Sumner immediately after the delivery of the celebrated oration, "The Scholar, the Artist, the Jurist, the Philanthropist," Mr. Adams remarks:—

"It is a gratification to me to have the opportunity to repeat the thanks which I so cordially gave you at the close of your oration last Thursday, and of which the sentiment offered by me at the dinner-table,* was but an additional pulsation from the same head. I trust I may now congratulate you on the felicity, first of your selection of your subject, and secondly, by its consummation in the delivery. But you will indulge me in the frankness and candor, which if they had not been the laws of a long life, would yet be imperative duties on its last stage, in the remark that the pleasure with which I listened to your discourse was inspired far less by the success, and all but universal acceptance and applause of the present moment, than by the vista of the future which it opened to my view. Casting my eyes back no further than the Fourth of July of the last year, when you set all the vipers of Alecto hissing, by proclaiming the Christian law of Universal Peace and Love, and then casting them forward perhaps, not much

* The sentiment was, — " The memory of the Scholar, the Jurist, the Artist, and the Philanthropist, and — not the memory, but the long life of the kindred spirit who has this day embalmed them all."

13

further, but beyond my own allotted time, I see you have a mission to perform. I look from Pisgah to the Promised Land, — you must enter upon it."

From Edward Everett.

The late Hon. Edward Everett, in acknowledging the receipt of the two-volume edition of Mr. Sumner's speeches, published several years ago, said : —

" Their contents, most of which were well known to me already, are among the most finished productions of their class in our language, — in any language. I am sure they will be read and admired, as long as anything English or American is remembered."

From Chancellor Kent, of New York.

Of Mr. Sumner's speech on " The Right of Search on the Coast of Africa," Chancellor Kent remarked in a private letter : —

" I have no hesitation in subscribing to it as entirely sound, logical, and conclusive. There is no doubt of it, and the neatness and elegance with which it is written are delightful."

The same eminent authority remarks of Mr. Sumner's Oration on " The True Grandeur of Nations," —

" I think the doctrine is well sustained by principle, and the precepts of the Gospel. The historical and classical illustrations are beautiful and apposite, and I cannot but think that such cogent and eloquent appeals to the heads and consciences of our people, must have effect."

Of Mr. Sumner's sketch of Hon. John Pickering, Chancellor Kent wrote : —

" The biographical sketch of that extraordinary scholar and man, John Pickering, is admirable, and most beautifully and eloquently drawn."

Of Mr. Sumner's celebrated " Phi Beta Kappa Address," he remarks : " I think it to be one of the most splendid productions, in point of diction and eloquence, that I have ever read."

From Martin Van Buren.

President Van Buren said of the oration on the "Law of Human Progress":—

"It has, be assured, afforded me the highest satisfaction to find a production affording such incontestable proof of the learning and great intellect of its author,—proceeding from a gentleman who has established the strongest claims to my admiration and respect."

From Judge Story.

Of Mr. Sumner's oration on "The True Grandeur of Nations," Judge Story remarked in a private letter:—

"It is certainly a very striking production, and will fully sustain Mr. Sumner's reputation for high talent, various reading, and exact scholarship. There are a great many passages in it which are wrought out with an exquisite finish, and elegance of diction, and classical style . . . . . In many parts of the discourse I have been struck with the strong resemblance which it bears to the manly, moral enthusiasm of Sir James Mackintosh."

From William Jay.

I have just received your very acceptable present,—acceptable from my esteem for the writer and for the great truths contained in the volumes, expressed with the elegance of the scholar and the fearless integrity of the Christian. When called to account for the use you have made of the talents intrusted to you, these volumes will testify that you have labored to do good in your day and generation.

In this connection the estimate entertained of Mr. Sumner by leading men in England, will be of interest. From the great multitude of similar opinions, the following are selected:—

From the Edinburgh Journal.

Mr. Sumner's lectures are not ordinary addresses,—they remind us rather of the orations of Demosthenes, of times when men of note, endowed with the highest understanding, gave full vent to the feelings that possessed them, and stirred their country with a fervid eloquence which was all the more impressive because it related to the political circumstances in which their country was placed.

We have in our possession many of Mr. Sumner's speeches, and we confess that, for depth and accuracy of thought, for fulness of historical information, and for a species of gigantic morality which treads all sophistry under foot, and rushes at once to the right conclusion, we know not a single orator, speaking the English tongue, who ranks as his superior. He combines, to a remarkable extent, the peculiar features of our British Emancipationists, the perseverance of Granville Sharpe, the knowledge of Brougham, the enthusiasm of Wilberforce, and a courage, which, as he is still a young man, may be expected to tell powerfully on the destinies of the Republic.

From Richard Cobden.

You have made the most noble contribution of any modern writer, to the cause of Peace.

From the London Examiner.

We would recommend a close and earnest study of the speech on the Fugitive Slave Act, made by Mr. Charles Sumner in the Senate of the United States on the 26th of last August (1852). That speech will reward perusal. Apart from its noble and effective eloquence, it is one of the closest and most convincing arguments we have ever read on the policy of the earlier and greater, as contrasted with that of the later and meaner, statesmen of America.

From a Letter of Lord Shaftesbury to the London Times.

Let us take a few lines descriptive of the terrible enactment from the speech of the Hon. Charles Sumner, one of those powerful intellects and noble hearts that have shone so brightly in our sister country, in the Senate of the United States. . . . . What noble eloquence! Carry these words, sir, by the vehicle of your almost universal paper to the press of every country, and to the heart of every human being — man, woman, or child — who has ever heard the divine rule, " Whatsoever ye would that men should do unto you, do ye even so to them."

From the Poet, Samuel Rogers.

In a letter to the author, the poet, Samuel Rogers, wrote: " What can I say to you in return for your admirable oration ? ('The True Grandeur of Nations.') I can only say with what pleasure I have read it, and how truly every pulse of my heart beats in accordance with yours on the subject. . . . . Again and again must I thank you."

———

From Lord Carlisle.

Lord Carlisle in his preface to an English edition of "Uncle Tom's Cabin," in some pleasant reminiscences of interviews with " my own most valued friend, Mr. Charles Sumner," remarks : —

" And now while I have been writing these lines, I have received the speech he has lately delivered in Congress on the bearings of the Fugitive Slave Law, which by the closeness of its logic, and the masculine vigor of its eloquence, proves to me how all the perfections of his mind have grown up to, and been dilated with the inspiration of the cause which he has now made his own.

———

From Chambers's Edinburgh Journal.

The oration (" The True Grandeur of Nations ") of Mr. Sumner, for taste, eloquence, and scholarship, as well as for fearless intrepidity, has been rarely equalled in modern harangues.

———

From the London Quarterly Review.

He presents in his own person a decisive proof that an American gentleman, without official rank or wide-spread reputation, by dint of courtesy, candor, an entire absence of pretension, an appreciative spirit, and a cultivated mind, may be received on a perfect footing of equality in the best circles, social, political, and intellectual, which, be it observed, are hopelessly inaccessible to the itinerant note-taker who never gets beyond the outskirts of the show-houses.